PENGUIN CLASSICS

THE GEORGICS

PUBLIUS VERGILIUS MARO was born on 15 October 70 BC, in a small village near Mantua in northern Italy. He wrote his *Ecologues* between 42 and 37 BC. Virgil began work on his second major poem, the *Georgics*, in 37 BC, under the urging of his patron, Maecenas; it was completed in 29 BC. Having gained the emperor's favour, Virgil was encouraged by Caesar Augustus to write a national epic celebrating Rome's glory. The *Aenid* was begun in 29 BC, but before it could be completed Virgil fell ill and died in 19 BC. He was buried near Naples.

KIMBERLY JOHNSON is a poet and scholar of Renaissance literature. She is the author of two collections of poetry, *Leviathan with a Hook* and *A Metaphorical God*, and is the recipient of a National Endowment for the Arts Creative Writing Fellowship. Her poems, essays and translations have appeared in numerous publications, including the *New Yorker*.

The Georgics

A Poem of the Land

Translated and edited by
KIMBERLY JOHNSON

PENGUIN BOOKS

For my parents
Te sine nil altum mens incohat.
(*Georgics* 3.42)

PENGUIN CLASSICS

Published by the Penguin Group
Penguin Books Ltd, 80 Strand, London WC2R 0RL, England
Penguin Group (USA) Inc., 375 Hudson Street, New York, New York 10014, USA
Penguin Group (Canada), 90 Eglinton Avenue East, Suite 700, Toronto, Ontario, Canada M4P 2Y3
(a division of Pearson Penguin Canada Inc.)
Penguin Ireland, 25 St Stephen's Green, Dublin 2, Ireland (a division of Penguin Books Ltd)
Penguin Group (Australia), 250 Camberwell Road, Camberwell, Victoria 3124, Australia
(a division of Pearson Australia Group Pty Ltd)
Penguin Books India Pvt Ltd, 11 Community Centre, Panchsheel Park, New Delhi – 110 017, India
Penguin Group (NZ), 67 Apollo Drive, Rosedale, North Shore 0632, New Zealand
(a division of Pearson New Zealand Ltd)
Penguin Books (South Africa) (Pty) Ltd, 24 Sturdee Avenue, Rosebank, Johannesburg 2196, South Africa

Penguin Books Ltd, Registered Offices: 80 Strand, London WC2R 0RL, England

www.penguin.com

This translation first published in Penguin Classics 2009
Published in paperback in Penguin Classics 2010

013

Translation and editorial material © Kimberly Johnson, 2009
All rights reserved

The moral right of the editor/translator has been asserted

Set in PostScript Adobe Sabon
Printed in Great Britain by Clays Ltd, Elcograf S.p.A.

ISBN: 978-0-140-45563-2

www.greenpenguin.co.uk

Contents

The Georgics:
A Poem of the Land

Acknowledgements

I am grateful to the editors of the following publications, in which sections of this translation, occasionally in different form, first appeared:

Arch Journal
Arion: A Journal of Humanities and the Classics
Circumference: Poetry in Translation
CutBank
The Diagram
Mantis: A Journal of Poetry, Criticism, and Translation
Metamorphoses: A Journal of Literary Translation
Natural Bridge
Sojourn
Southern Humanities Review
Translation: A Translation Studies Journal
Two Lines: A Journal of Translation

Thanks to Peter Carson, Alexis Kirschbaum, Ian Pindar, and all at Penguin, and especially to A. E. Stallings for speeding the plough. For the interest they have shown in this project from its earliest days, I would like to express my gratitude to Paul Alpers, Donald M. Friedman, Kevis Goodman, Robert Hass and John Talbot. Lawrence Revard provided invaluable feedback on some particularly tricky lines, as did Charles Henderson (though he did so without knowing my identity). Michael Greenfield read thoughtfully and responded to early drafts. My greatest debt I acknowledge in this book's dedication.

Chronology

He completes the *Eclogues* and begins work on the *Georgics*.
Varro publishes his *Res Rusticae* (*On Rural Matters*)

31 Octavian, with his general Agrippa, defeats his former ally
Mark Antony and Cleopatra at Actium, defying once and for
all his challengers

30 Mark Antony dies. Publication of Horace's *Epodes*

29 Virgil finishes the *Georgics* and begins work on the *Aeneid*

27 Octavian becomes Emperor and takes the name Caesar
Augustus. Livy begins publishing his *Ab Urbe Condita* (literally, *From the Founding of the City*), his history of Rome

23 Publication of Horace's *Odes*, Books 1–3

20 Virgil meets Caesar Augustus in Athens and accompanies
him to Megara

19 On 21 September Virgil dies of a fever contracted during his
travels in Greece. His *Aeneid* is published posthumously

18 Horace publishes his *Ars Poetica* (*The Art of Poetry*)

16 Ovid publishes the *Amores* (*The Loves*)

AD

8 Ovid publishes the *Metamorphoses*

14 Death of Caesar Augustus

Introduction

Virgil's Life and Art

Publius Vergilius Maro was born on 15 October, 70 BC, in a small village in northern Italy, near Mantua, an ancient city on the banks of the River Mincius. His father was a man of humble means – a labourer, or perhaps a craftsman who made earthenware pots – who married a woman of higher social status, the daughter of his employer. Virgil was sent with children of higher social status to be educated in Cremona during his early teens, and from there continued his education in Mediolanum (modern Milan), which was then the intellectual and cultural centre of northern Italy. He went on to Rome at age seventeen, considering a career in the law, but his native shyness and reluctant tongue seem to have frustrated his intentions. He spoke in court only once.

A life of the mind proved more congenial to Virgil. While at Rome he was deeply influenced by Epicurean philosophy and he later removed from Rome to join the quiet, seaside Epicurean colony run by the philosopher Siro (*c.* 50 BC) in Parthenope (in modern Naples). His reading during this time certainly included Lucretius (*c.* 95–*c.* 55 BC), whose recently published *De Rerum Natura* (*On the Nature of Things*) exemplified the Epicurean values of temperance, the pursuit of knowledge and simple living. Virgil learned Greek and read widely in the works of Hesiod (*c.* 700 BC) and Theocritus (*c.* 308–*c.* 240 BC). It was here that he spent the five-year period of the first Roman civil war, in which Julius Caesar (100–44 BC) opposed and eventually defeated the forces of Pompey (106–48 BC) and the Roman Senate (49–45 BC).

Though Virgil was probably not actively involved in Julius Caesar's war, he became more invested in the political fortunes of Caesar's successor. After Caesar was assassinated in 44 BC, the republican troops led by Marcus Junius Brutus (85–42 BC) and Gaius Cassius Longinus (c. 85–42 BC) were defeated by followers of Caesar, led by Mark Antony (83–30 BC) and the fallen emperor's adopted son Octavian (63 BC–AD 14). Octavian rewarded the soldiers under his command with gifts of land, which had been commandeered from towns and villages in northern Italy – including Virgil's native Mantua. Virgil's family property seems not to have been among the properties reassigned to war veterans. Sometime around 41 BC the poet returned to his family's farm to help care for his aging parents and their land, and to write.

His first major work was the *Eclogues*. Composed between 42 and 37 BC, these ten pastoral poems represent a series of conversations between rustic characters, shepherds and peasants who offer commentary (sometimes oblique) about contemporary politics. Most topically, the two speakers of Eclogue 1, Tityrus and Meliboeus, discuss the plight of dispossessed landholders. But the songs and dialogues of these poems take place in the remove of rural peace, and their pastoral settings offer an ideal against which the tensions of politics and the city seem poor indeed. The *Eclogues* are modelled in their form and style after the Είδύλλια (*Idylls*) of Theocritus, which were written during the third century BC, and indicate Virgil's mounting determination to refashion the conventions of Greek literature and claim its poetic legacy for Rome.

After he had completed the *Eclogues*, Virgil commenced work on his great middle poem, the *Georgics*. He had, by the time of the *Eclogues'* publication, gained the patronage of Gaius Maecenas (d. 8 BC), a wealthy and influential Roman and capable advisor to Octavian. It was at the insistence of Maecenas that Virgil began work on the *Georgics*; Maecenas actively cultivated the favour of writers, partly in an effort to direct public sympathies toward Octavian in anticipation of his imperial bid. During the seven years Virgil spent toiling over the *Georgics*, he resided in Naples and continued to enjoy the influence of the Epicurean community there. His reading led him back again to Lucretius, and beyond: to Hesiod's Ἔργα καὶ Ἡμέραι (*Works and Days*), which, like the *Georgics*, imagines a Golden Age filled with peace and free from labour; to the *Res Rusticae* (*On Rural Matters*) by Marcus Terentius Varro (116–27 BC), whose three books are devoted, respectively, to agriculture, cattle and smaller farm animals like poultry, game birds and bees; to the Φαινόμενα or *Phaeno-mena* (*Sky-Sightings*) by Aratus (*c.* 315–240 BC), a poem about the weather, astronomy and sky-signs; to Cato (234–149 BC) and to Callimachus (*c.* 305–*c.* 240 BC).

Octavian – soon to become Caesar Augustus – seems to have rewarded Virgil's praise by showing him preferment. Virgil's ancient biographers Servius (late fourth century AD) and Suetonius (*c.* AD 69–*c.* 140) tell us that once the poet had completed work on the poem in 29 BC he read it aloud to Octavian, who was returning triumphant from the Battle of Actium (31 BC). When Virgil's voice grew tired, Maecenas took over. Octavian was sufficiently impressed with the *Georgics* that he pressed Virgil to undertake a poem that would celebrate the glory of Rome. In response, Virgil began the *Aeneid*.

In this last great work, the poet sets forth to relate the ancient legacy of the Roman state. Virgil describes the founding of Rome by Aeneas, a survivor of the sack of Troy, who is guided by the gods to the Italian shores, heroically overcoming diffi-culties along the way, to establish a glorious new empire. Virgil worked on the *Aeneid* for the last ten years of his life. He planned to continue revising and adding to his epic, but con-tracted an illness during an extended period of travel through Greece. Virgil cut his journey short and headed back to Italy, where he died after arriving in Brundisium (modern Brindisi), in southern Italy. His great epic was left unfinished.

Virgil had left instructions with his friend, the poet Lucius Varius Rufus (*c.* 74–14 BC), to destroy his manuscript if he did not return to perfect it. We learn, again from Suetonius, that Caesar Augustus prevented Virgil's wishes from being carried out, and ordered that the unfinished manuscript be published.

Virgil was buried near his beloved Naples, under a stone bearing an epitaph he had composed himself:

> *Mantua me genuit, Calabri rapuere, tenet nunc*
> *Parthenope; cecini pascua, rura, duces.*

> Mantua bore me, Calabria seized me, now Naples
> holds me. I have sung of pastures, the land and kings.

On Virgil's Georgics: *The Work of Art*

To work the earth: this is the deepest etymological meaning of the word 'georgic', deriving from ancient Greek γή or 'earth', and ἔργον or 'work'. The close historical association between Virgil's middle poem and agriculture has nearly obviated any need for commentary on the subject. The *Georgics* seems, irreducibly, and even in its title, to be a long poem about working the earth in order to reap its manifold bounties, and it includes instruction on maintaining grain crops, wine and the olive, herds and flocks, as well as bees. If we were to take Virgil's agricultural subjects at face value we might be tempted to consider the *Georgics* a sort of *Farmer's Almanac* in verse, a bit of a literary oddity – sociologically interesting, perhaps, for the way it illuminates the farmhand's practice of two millennia ago, but ultimately lacking the epic reach of the poet's later work, the *Aeneid*, or the dramatic verve of his earlier pastoral work, the *Eclogues*.

But the poem does not encourage us, either as readers or as potential rustic pupils, to consider the *Georgics* as a didactic agricultural poem. Although its four books purport to provide instruction in a number of agricultural methods and techniques, in practical terms Virgil's guidelines fall somewhat short of reliability. More accurate agricultural manuals – like Varro's *Res Rusticae* and Aratus' *Phaenomena* – were already available in Virgil's Rome, and his poem reflects a knowledge of those texts, although his incorporation of their subject matter does not suggest that he felt any obligation to stay true to their teachings. In fact, the *Georgics* subverts its instruction-manual stance with sly frequency, as when in Book Four he prescribes the manifest fiction of *bugonia* – the spontaneous generation of insects in an ox carcass – to remedy a failed beehive (see 4.281–558).

Given the poem's simultaneous assertion of and undermining of its own rustic authority, how are we to understand the project of Virgil's lovely and strange achievement? For certainly, the *Georgics* is an achievement: expansive in its scope, complexly structured with lush and challenging language, by turns realistic and fantastic, elevated and earthy, wistful and pragmatic. Its literary allusions are dizzying, almost impossible to account for in full – a feature which establishes Virgil's venture as a primarily poetic and literary one. But the texts to which he alludes are both poetic – including Homer (probably eighth century BC) and Callimachus – *and* instructive, such as Varro and Aratus, and the Περὶ φυτικῶν ἱστοριῶν or *Historia Plantarum* (*History of Plants*) by Theophrastus (?372–?288 BC). By bringing together elements that would seem to be in opposition, the *Georgics* emphasizes variegation and experimentation, a position that revises the definitive authority of the traditional agricultural manual, promoting ambiguity and uncertainty in place of didactic conviction.

The poem's investment in ambiguity and uncertainty is most apparent in its treatment of work. Work, the labour of man, stands as the dominant subject of Virgil's text, from the title onward. Indeed, the first five lines of the poem announce that labour is the thematic motivation for the *Georgics*:

> Quid faciat laetas segetes, quo sidere terram
> vertere, Maecenas, ulmisque adiungere vites
> conveniat, quae cura boum, qui cultus habendo
> sit pecori, apibus quanta experientia parcis,
> hinc canere incipiam.

> What cheers the grain, beneath what star to turn
> the soil, Maecenas, when to wed vines
> to the elms, what care the cows, what care
> the flocks require, what skill the thrifty bees, –
> here I begin my song. (1.1–5)

These introductory lines lay out in order the topics of the
Georgics' four books, and Virgil does proceed through each of
these subjects in turn, careful in each case to describe the labour
required to produce a good yield. The good ploughman must,
we are told in Book One, break up the soil, rotate crops, irrigate,
make tight the threshing-floor and sharpen his ploughshare
indoors on stormy evenings, among other things. The would-be
vintner must cultivate the wild acres, make use of budding and
grafting techniques, plant vines and trees in soil appropriate to
their needs, dig the earth and keep it weeded. The herdsman
must be attentive in his breeding and plan for the future of the
herd, train his animals to the tasks they will undertake, guard
against the beasts' instinctive but strength-sapping lusts, and
take measures to drive out pestilence and predators. The bee-
keeper must find a location amenable to bees and plant it with
aromatic vegetation, control their tiny conflicts, harvest honey
and keep the hive in good repair.

All these pursuits require human labour, and Virgil specifies
the pains that should be taken. The beekeeper is instructed to
exert considerable effort by his own hand:

> ipse thymum pinosque ferens de montibus altis
> tecta serat late circum, cui talia curae;
> ipse labore manum duro terat, ipse feracis
> figat humo plantas et amicos inriget imbris.

> Let him whose care they are himself fetch thyme and pines
> from mountain peaks, and plant them round about their lodge,
> himself callous his hand with rugged work, himself plant
> fruitful slips in the soil and water them with kind sprinklings.

> (4.112–15)

The repetition of 'ipse' ('himself') conveys with some insistence
that the exertion of personal labour is essential to the poem's
vision of apiary success. Likewise, the cattleman is counselled
to feed the young steers 'frumenta manu carpes sata' or '*hand-
plucked* grain' (3.176), a task shared by the dairy shepherd:

> At cui lactis amor, cytisum lotosque frequentis
> ipse manu salsasque ferat praesepibus herbas.

> But let him who loves milk fetch to the stalls
> lotus and clover by his own hand, and salted feed ...
>
> (3.394–5)

Virgil's admonition to the viticulturist in Book Two may appear to echo down the entirety of the poem: 'Scilicet omnibus est labor impendendus', 'To all, of course, apply your labours' (2.61).

Despite the text's repeated directive to labour, the *Georgics* expresses a deep ambivalence about the efficacy of work. In the world of the *Georgics*, labour is as likely to fail as it is to succeed. Early on in the poem, Virgil tells us that, even though 'seasoned men and oxen struggle thus / to turn the soil' (1.118–19), yet the world at large endangers the ploughman's efforts. The centrepiece of the first book describes the violence of a crop-killing storm, in which

> omnia ventorum concurrere proelia ...
> quae gravidam late segetem ab radicibus imis
> sublimem expulsam eruerent ...

> ... all the armies of wind clash
> uprooting plump grain left and right from deepest roots
> and hurling it high ... (1.318–20)

All the struggles of those seasoned men and oxen are no match for the ravages of the natural world, which in addition to weather include weeds, sickness, shade and a host of animal pests. Book One ends with the image of a charioteer sawing away at his reins in vain while his coursers thunder on, ignoring his exertions. In Book Four the industrious, anthropomorphic bees are susceptible to 'grim disease' (4.252), and the long closing sequence retelling the story of Orpheus is initiated in response to the failure of a hive – a calamity whose repair lies strictly in the realm of the mythic. And in Book Three the herdsman contends with the natures of the animals themselves, going to great lengths to keep cattle and horses from rutting their strength away, efforts which ultimately prove pointless before the devastations of disease. Against this threat, men slaughter animals to prevent the spread of sickness – hardly a satisfying solution. But after Virgil has urged various treatments for the diseased flock, he turns immediately to the plague, an irremediable sickness so fierce that it flummoxes even the gods:

> saepe in honore deum medio stans hostia ad aram,
> lanea dum nivea circumdatur infula vitta,
> inter cunctantis cecidit moribunda ministros.
> aut si quam ferro mactaverat ante sacerdos,
> inde neque impositis ardent altaria fibris,
> nec responsa potest consultus reddere vates . . .

> Often in the middle of oblations for the gods, the victim waiting
>   at the altar,
> the woollen fillet with its snow-white garland circling its brow,
> dropped dead among the dawdling ministrants.
> Or even if, before it succumbed, the priest slaughtered with his
>   blade,
> neither did the altars blaze from the entrails laid upon,
> nor could the oracle implored return an explanation. (3.486–91)

The plague sequence supplies the poem's most vivid language, its most locomotive pacing, and marshals these strengths in the service of a fearsome example of the utter impotence of labour.

Even successful labour, the kind idealized by so many parts of the *Georgics*, is viewed at times with a determined optimism. For the *Georgics* is situated firmly in the world of work by necessity, as a consequence of the earth's fall from the idyllic age of the reign of Saturn to the demands of the reign of Jupiter. 'Before Jove,' Virgil tells us, 'no yeoman groomed the soil' (1.125). But after his overthrow of Saturn, the golden world was changed, as almighty Jupiter

> ... malum virus serpentibus addidit atris,
> praedarique lupos iussit pontumque moveri,
> mellaque decussit foliis, ignemque removit
> et passim rivis currentia vina repressit,
> ut varias usus meditando extunderet artis ...

> put dire venom into vipers black, bade wolves
> to raven and the sea to heave, shook honey from the leaves,
> secreted fire, stanched the wine that ran everywhere in streams,
> so that need with contemplation might forge sundry arts ...
>   (1.129–33)

Here, Virgil acknowledges that invention and discovery – what we might call 'progress' – do occur as a result of man's compulsory labour, but the incentive seems closer to desperation than to inspiration when the poet summarizes the driving force behind the workman's dedication this way:

> ... sic omnia fatis
> in peius ruere ac retro sublapsa referri,
> non aliter, quam qui adverso vix flumine lembum
> remigiis subigit, si bracchia forte remisit,
> atque illum in praeceps prono rapit alveus amni.

> ... So by decree
> all things incline to worse, and foundering backslide, back
> like one whose oar can scarcely thrust his skiff upstream;
> if perchance he slack his arms, sternward
> the coursing water drags him down the rapids. (1.199–203)

Throughout the *Georgics* there is a pervasive sense that humanity's gains by way of labour offer small compensation for the striveless paradise lost, the fellowship of man and nature before the fall of Saturn, the innocence of that golden time before 'departing Justice left her last footprints upon the earth' (2.474).

Given the poem's bumper crop of mixed messages, it may be most accurate to say that the labour advocated most persistently in the *Georgics* is that of interpretation. The reader, faced with the text's strategies of divergence, must endeavour to reconcile opposites, to synthesize coherence out of apparent contradiction. This work occurs, as we have seen, in the poem's presentation of often opposing arguments, but also in its complex structure, and in the metrical tension it creates between the natural stress of words and the demands of Virgil's Greek-influenced quantitative hexameter. We labour, too, as readers, to hear the echoes of other texts in Virgil's many allusions, but must frequently abandon those former texts as soon as we identify their echoes, because the *Georgics* so aggressively appropriates its source texts, revising them to create new associations and concerns. We toil to follow the poem's negotiation of the cultural value of art, its ambivalent politics, its slightly sceptical piety. In short, we must tackle an unexpectedly broad range of knowledge in order to comprehend this little agricultural handbook.

Virgil thematizes the labour of reading throughout the poem. Book One provides a virtual primer for interpreting the world's legible signs. 'We must watch the stars,' he tells us at 1.204, to determine the right times to plant. And the moon. And the sun. And the weather, the wind, the birds and ants, the walnut tree in the woods – as if the whole earth were a book that, if accurately read, would spell only bounty. The vintage depends on the vintner's acumen at soil-reading. The vigour of the flock needs the shepherd's trained interpretation of disease's signals. The hive thrives only when the beekeeper can discern the marks of weakness and breed them out. The sheer accumulation of these decoding tips suggests that decoding is, itself, the crucial activity; in the *Georgics* all other skills are contingent on the skill of interpretation – a notion borne out in its first five lines, where the tasks of husbandry to be described are all contingent upon the fifth line: 'hinc canere incipiam', 'here I begin my song'. (The poet, who perceives his material and organizes it into coherence, is a reader too.) This realization prompts a revision of our sense of the poem's didacticism: the *Georgics'* most persistent instruction seems to lie in educating its *reader* in the essential – and difficult – task of interpretation.

Perhaps the poem's stake in intricate reading is rooted ulti-
mately in the cultural moment of the *Georgics*' production.
Virgil composed the *Georgics* over a seven-year period, from
36 to 29 BC, so the work would have been begun less than a
decade after the uncomfortable resolution of the Roman civil
war, when Julius Caesar defeated the supporters of Pompey at
Pharsalus. Rome emerged from this first civil war only to enter
into another, following Caesar's assassination, which pitted his
heir Octavian and his ally Mark Antony against Brutus and the
forces of republicanism. Though Octavian gained the triumph,
the predictable rivalry between Antony and Octavian flared
into yet another conflict, which culminated in the defeat of
Antony's (and Cleopatra's) forces at Actium in 31 BC.

Virgil observed this political turmoil from an unsettled pos-
ition. On one hand, he had gained the patronage of Maecenas,
a member of Octavian's circle of advisers, and enjoyed the kind
of security that attends an established regime. On the other
hand, as his first *Eclogue* indicates, the poet clearly harboured
real unease about the seizure of rural land, including properties
in his native province of Mantua, and its reassignment to war
veterans. Virgil's political ambivalence surfaces in the conflict-
ing gestures which litter the *Georgics*, as in the contrast between
Book Two's famed *laudes Italiae*, or the praises of Italy, which
number among Italy's glories her 'warhorses charg[ing] haughty
on the field' (2.145), and the indictment that closes Book One,
where Italy's sins include that she gives 'No rightful honour to
the plough; the croppers commandeered, / soil weeds to rot; and
hooked sickles are forged to rigid swords' (1.508–9). Virgil's
divided perspective will find fuller expression in the *Aeneid*,
whose epic drama produces a glorious national myth, but at
the same time imagines that myth in the distant past, its long
legacy a fading benchmark for Virgil's Rome to recover.

Virgil's dual strategies of praise and reproach do more than
reflect the myriad contrasting concerns of the poem; they also
create in the *Georgics* a world of interpretive instability, of
contradictions and digressions and disunity, despite the over-
arching agricultural narrative. In this context, reading becomes

not merely an information-harvesting machine but a means of repair, a process by which the ramshackle world is organized, made comprehensible – literally, made *legible*. We might say that Virgil offers his reader a poetic version of his own times, filled with struggle and disrepair, difficulty and ambiguity, uncertainties and shifting allegiances. The poem is complicated. It is our appointed labour, as readers, to work toward comprehension, to find in the turning furrows of Virgil's lines a unified field.

But even this task is not without its snares. At several points in the *Georgics*, Virgil describes the work of interpretation as a kind of conquest, a campaign to parallel the battlefield exploits of Caesar. Virgil vaunts that he will 'sing through Roman plazas the song of Ascra' (2.176), appropriating the position of Hesiod, and envisions himself seizing the glories of ancient Greece for Rome (see 3.8–20) – a plan of action he carries out throughout the text by commandeering and redeploying pieces of Greek literature. These boasts of poetic occupation comment cannily on the real dangers of the work of empire: uniting the disparate and encompassing the manifold can very easily turn to strong-arming a cohesive whole. Once again, we find the *Georgics* making its stand on ambivalence. By positing interpretive divergences, the poem encourages the reader to do the work of reconciling, but undermines the principle of resolution by suggesting that forced assimilation, even of texts, is a form of conquest.

The ethical difficulties that attend acts of interpretation were as familiar to Virgil as they should be to us in our postmodern context. If the *Georgics* is didactic about anything, then, perhaps it is in the hermeneutic lesson it demands its reader to learn, about the patient and fraught work of synthesis, about the challenge of locating unity without imposing unanimity. In this light, the *Georgics* offers its reader a striking exercise in the cultivation and control of the greedy domain of the mind. It is a poem for a time of empire.

It is a poem for our time.

Further Reading

Abbe, Elfriede, *The Plants of Virgil's* Georgics (Ithaca: Cornell University Press, 1965).

Boyle, A. J. (ed.), *Virgil's Ascraean Song:* Ramus *essays on the* Georgics (Berwick, Victoria: Aureal Publications, 1979).

Feeney, Denis C., *Literature and Religion at Rome: Cultures, Contexts, and Beliefs* (Cambridge: Cambridge University Press, 1998).

Fraser, H. Malcolm, *Beekeeping in Antiquity* (London: University of London Press, 1931).

Goodman, Kevis, *Georgic Modernity and British Romanticism: Poetry and the Mediation of History* (Cambridge: Cambridge University Press, 2004).

Jermyn, L. A. S., 'Weather-signs in Vergil', *Greece and Rome* 20 (1951), pp. 26–37, 49–59.

Nelson, Stephanie A., *God and the Land: The Metaphysics of Farming in Hesiod and Vergil* (New York: Oxford University Press, 1998).

O'Hara, James J., *True Names: Vergil and the Alexandrian Tradition of Etymological Wordplay* (Ann Arbor: University of Michigan Press, 1996).

Putnam, Michael C. J., *Virgil's Poem of the Earth: Studies in the* Georgics (Princeton: Princeton University Press, 1979).

Ross, David O., *Virgil's Elements: Physics and Poetry in the* Georgics (Princeton: Princeton University Press, 1987).

Royds, T. F., *The Beasts, Birds and Bees of Virgil* (Oxford: Blackwell, 1914).

Sargeaunt, John, *The Trees, Shrubs, and Plants of Virgil* (Oxford: Blackwell, 1920).

Syme, Ronald, *The Roman Revolution* (Oxford: Clarendon Press, 1939).

Thomas, Richard F., *Reading Virgil and His Texts: Studies in Intertextuality* (Ann Arbor: University of Michigan Press, 1999).

—— (ed.), *Virgil*, Georgics (2 volumes). Cambridge Greek and Latin Classics (Cambridge: Cambridge University Press, 1988).

White, K. D., *Agricultural Implements of the Roman World* (Cambridge: Cambridge University Press, 1967).

——, *Farm Equipment of the Roman World* (Cambridge: Cambridge University Press, 1975).

——, *Roman Farming* (Ithaca: Cornell University Press, 1970).

Wilkinson, L. P., *The Georgics of Virgil: A Critical Survey* (Cambridge: Cambridge University Press, 1969).

Translator's Note

The earliest major sources for Virgil's Latin *Georgics* are manuscripts surviving from the fourth and fifth centuries AD. They include

- the *Codex Romanus* or *Vergilius Romanus*, containing the *Eclogues*, *Georgics* and *Aeneid*, with few missing pages;
- the *Codex Palatinus* or *Palatinus Vaticanus*, a fourth- or fifth-century text also containing the entirety of Virgil's corpus, with few missing pages;
- the *Codex Mediceus* at Florence, dating from the late 400s, which includes the whole of the *Georgics*;
- the *Schedae Vaticanae* or *Vergilius Vaticanus*, containing much of Books Three and Four.

Other early manuscript sources contain smaller fragments of the text:

- the *Schedae Vaticano-Berolinenses*, which includes sections of Books One and Three;
- the *Schedae Sangallenses*, which contains portions of Book Four; and
- the *Schedae rescriptae Veronenses*, a palimpsest in fragments.

The first authoritative edition of Virgil's work appeared in Rome in the late fifteenth century, around the same time that the fourth-century commentaries on Virgil by Servius were published.

Authoritative modern editions of the Latin *Georgics* include
R. A. B. Mynors (ed.) *P. Vergili Maronis opera* (Oxford: Oxford
Classical Text, 1972) and Marius Geymonat (ed.), *P. Vergili
Maronis opera* (Turin: Paravia, 1973). These modern editions
differ occasionally, but their departures from one another tend
to be of the minor variety; most frequently, they are differences
in punctuation.

This translation maintains no firm manuscript allegiance,
though it adheres for the most part to the Latin text as it
appears in Mynors. Since most manuscript discrepancies are
minor, this translation passes by many of them without com-
ment. However, when manuscript variances present substantial
differences in interpretation this translation addresses those
variances in its Notes section, explaining in each case the con-
tested word or phrase and accounting for the present volume's
textual decision. I have been aided greatly throughout the pro-
cess of translation by Richard F. Thomas's two-volume com-
mentary on the poem (see Further Reading).

Many English translations of the *Georgics* elect to render its
hexameter lines in prose, recognizing that it is nearly impossible
to approximate in English the quantitative metre of Virgil's
Latin (which measures its lines according to the length of syl-
lables). Other translations, following perhaps the model of John
Dryden's influential seventeenth-century rendering of the poem,
use iambic pentameter, which traditionally has been thought –
because of its stately pace and suggestiveness of the natural
human breath-span – to provide a rough equivalent of dactylic
hexameter. This translation departs from those conventions,
adopting instead a loose metre most reminiscent, perhaps, of
Gerard Manley Hopkins's 'sprung rhythm', with five to six
stressed positions in each line. This strategy is meant to
acknowledge the dynamic quality of Virgil's lines, in which the
metrical structure asserts itself in counterpoint to the natural
stress of individual words. It also enacts the agility of the origi-
nal metre, which allowed the unstressed position to be occupied
by either a single syllable *or* two syllables.

This translation has made a particular effort to replicate
the syntactic experience of reading Virgil's Latin, to preserve

original structure as far as possible. Although this occasionally results in English sentences that require slower reading, it does go some way toward preserving the linear accumulation of detail in the poem – an important consideration in a work so conscious of the ordering of labour. Moreover, Virgil's attention to the etymological connection between poetry and ploughing – contained in the roots of the word 'verse', *vertere*, to turn – recommends at least some endeavour on the part of the translator to sow the details of language in order, so that they can be reaped with their original associations intact.

The *Georgics* also works to activate the reader's physical participation in the text by means of sonic effects beyond metre. Where the sound of language is itself an obvious vector of communication I have attempted to translate sound-for-sound, as when, in Book Two, Virgil describes the tongue-turning taste of bitter soil – and forces the reader to spit out *t* sounds and *s* sounds repeatedly, as if in sympathetic distaste:

> . . . sapor indicium faciet manifestus, et ora
> tristia temptantum sensu torquebit amaro.

> . . . its taste will testify, its bitter tang
> will twist the taster's bittered tongue. (2.246–7)

These concerns about the work's extralexical elements, central to any discussion of poetry, are particularly resonant in the *Georgics*. The *Georgics* is, after all, a profoundly human work and its poetic engagement of the body, its dense and complex music, assists in the poem's educative programme by implicating the reader sensorily, as well as instructively, in its unfolding scheme.

A POEM OF THE LAND:
THE *GEORGICS*

Book One

LIBER I

Quid faciat laetas segetes, quo sidere terram
vertere, Maecenas, ulmisque adiungere vites
conveniat, quae cura boum, qui cultus habendo
sit pecori, apibus quanta experientia parcis,
hinc canere incipiam. vos, o clarissima mundi
lumina, labentem caelo quae ducitis annum,
Liber et alma Ceres, vestro si munere tellus
Chaoniam pingui glandem mutavit arista,
poculaque inventis Acheloia miscuit uvis;
et vos, agrestum praesentia numina, Fauni,
(ferte simul Faunique pedem Dryadesque puellae!)
munera vestra cano. tuque o, cui prima frementem
fudit equum magno tellus percussa tridenti,
Neptune; et cultor nemorum, cui pinguia Ceae
ter centum nivei tondent dumeta iuvenci;
ipse, nemus linquens patrium saltusque Lycaei,
Pan, ovium custos, tua si tibi Maenala curae,
adsis, o Tegeaee, favens, oleaeque Minerva
inventrix, uncique puer monstrator aratri,
et teneram ab radice ferens, Silvane, cupressum,
dique deaeque omnes, studium quibus arva tueri,
quique novas alitis non ullo semine fruges,
quique satis largum caelo demittitis imbrem.
tuque adeo, quem mox quae sint habitura deorum
concilia, incertum est, urbisne invisere, Caesar,
terrarumque velis curam et te maximus orbis

BOOK ONE

What cheers the grain, beneath what star to turn
the soil, Maecenas, when to wed vines
to the elms, what care the cows, what care
the flocks require, what skill the thrifty bees, –
here I begin my song. You, O brightest fires
of heaven, that guide the gliding year across the sky,
you, O Liber and generous Ceres, if by your influence earth
changed Chaonian acorns for sumptuous corn
and steeped new grapes in drafts of Achelous;
and you, the bumpkin's practical gods, you Fauns   10
(lift steps together, Fauns and wood-maids!),
your bounties I sing. O Neptune, you – for whom the
    ground
hammered by your mighty trident first cast forth
the champing horse; and you, the genius of the groves,
whose three hundred snowy bullocks crop
the lush thickets of Cea; and you yourself, Tegean Pan,
careful shepherd, forsaking your native glades
and woods of Lycaeus and your loved Maenalus,
kindly come. Come Minerva, who contrived the olive,
come swain who trained us in the curving plough,
and Silvanus with your uprooted cypress sapling, all gods   20
and goddesses who keep watch over fields –
you who nurse the tender, unsown fruits, who pour
from heaven lavish rain. And chiefly you,
O Caesar, whom unknown assemblies of gods may claim
in time, whether you choose to survey cities
and succour lands while all the world declares you

auctorem frugum tempestatumque potentem
accipiat, cingens materna tempora myrto,
an deus inmensi venias maris ac tua nautae
30   numina sola colant, tibi serviat ultima Thule,
teque sibi generum Tethys emat omnibus undis,
anne novum tardis sidus te mensibus addas,
qua locus Erigonen inter Chelasque sequentis
panditur (ipse tibi iam bracchia contrahit ardens
Scorpius et caeli iusta plus parte reliquit):
quidquid eris (nam te nec sperant Tartara regem
nec tibi regnandi veniat tam dira cupido,
quamvis Elysios miretur Graecia campos
nec repetita sequi curet Proserpina matrem),
40   da facilem cursum atque audacibus adnue coeptis
ignarosque viae mecum miseratus agrestis
ingredere et votis iam nunc adsuesce vocari.

Vere novo, gelidus canis cum montibus umor
liquitur et Zephyro putris se glaeba resolvit,
depresso incipiat iam tum mihi taurus aratro
ingemere, et sulco attritus splendescere vomer.
illa seges demum votis respondet avari
agricolae, bis quae solem, bis frigora sensit;
illius immensae ruperunt horrea messes.
50   at prius ignotum ferro quam scindimus aequor,
ventos et varium caeli praediscere morem
cura sit ac patrios cultusque habitusque locorum,
et quid quaeque ferat regio et quid quaeque recuset.
hic segetes, illic veniunt felicius uvae,
arborei fetus alibi, atque iniussa virescunt
gramina. nonne vides, croceos ut Tmolus odores,
India mittit ebur, molles sua tura Sabaei,
at Chalybes nudi ferrum, virosaque Pontus
castorea, Eliadum palmas Epiros equarum.
60   continuo has leges aeternaque foedera certis

author of increase and master of skies and wreathes
your brows with your bright mother's myrtles,
or whether you appear a god of the unfathomable sea
as sailors reverence your glory alone and farthest Thule   30
serves you, and Tethys with all her waves
bids for your seed, or whether you bestow yourself
a new star to the languid months
where between the Virgin and the claws that chase her
a space is opening (already the ardent Scorpion
contracts his arms to yield you greater share of heaven) . . .
Whatever you will be (– but Tartarus hopes not for you
as its king – and never may such cruel lust for dominion
come upon you, though Greece reveres Elysian Fields
and Persephone reclaimed complains to surface with her
        mother),
make smooth my course, approve my bold endeavour,   40
and, pitying with me peasants unknowing of the way,
step up and learn even now to honour prayers.

In new spring, when from snowy peaks the run-off
flows, and the mouldering clod crumbles under the Zephyr,
straightaway I'd hitch my bull to groan before the deep-
driven plough, its blade scoured to gleaming by the furrow.
That field alone fulfils the keen farmer's prayer
which twice sun and twice frost has felt:
its teeming harvests burst the granaries.
But before our iron carves an unknown plain,   50
let our study be to learn its winds and fickle sky,
the local tricks, the temper of the land,
what each zone yields, what each refuses.
Here corn, there grapes will sprout more exuberantly,
there fruited trees, or herbs unbidden flourish.
See how Tmolus offers up saffron fumes,
India sends ivory, and the soft Sabaeans incense,
but the bare Chalybes export iron, Pontus the pungent
        musk
of beavers, and Epirus the palms of Olympian mares?
From the first has Nature fixed for discrete climes   60

imposuit natura locis, quo tempore primum
Deucalion vacuum lapides iactavit in orbem,
unde homines nati, durum genus. ergo age, terrae
pingue solum primis extemplo a mensibus anni
fortes invertant tauri, glaebasque iacentis
pulverulenta coquat maturis solibus aestas;
at si non fuerit tellus fecunda, sub ipsum
Arcturum tenui sat erit suspendere sulco:
illic, officiant laetis ne frugibus herbae,
70 hic, sterilem exiguus ne deserat umor harenam.

Alternis idem tonsas cessare novalis
et segnem patiere situ durescere campum;
aut ibi flava seres mutato sidere farra,
unde prius laetum siliqua quassante legumen
aut tenuis fetus viciae tristisque lupini
sustuleris fragilis calamos silvamque sonantem.
urit enim lini campum seges, urit avenae,
urunt Lethaeo perfusa papavera somno;
sed tamen alternis facilis labor, arida tantum
80 ne saturare fimo pingui pudeat sola neve
effetos cinerem inmundum iactare per agros.
sic quoque mutatis requiescunt fetibus arva,
nec nulla interea est inaratae gratia terrae.
saepe etiam sterilis incendere profuit agros
atque levem stipulam crepitantibus urere flammis:
sive inde occultas vires et pabula terrae
pinguia concipiunt, sive illis omne per ignem
excoquitur vitium atque exsudat inutilis umor,
seu pluris calor ille vias et caeca relaxat
90 spiramenta, novas veniat qua sucus in herbas,
seu durat magis et venas adstringit hiantis,
ne tenues pluviae rapidive potentia solis
acrior aut Boreae penetrabile frigus adurat.
multum adeo, rastris glaebas qui frangit inertis
vimineasque trahit cratis, iuvat arva, neque illum
flava Ceres alto nequiquam spectat Olympo;

these laws and compacts everlasting, from the moment
Deucalion sowed stones upon the empty world
from which sprang men, a gritty race. Up then, where soil
is rich make haste and let your oxen hale upturn it
in the year's first months, then let the clods lie
for dusty summer to bake with ripening suns.
But if your earth's not fertile, it will do
to furrow up a shallow ridge as Arcturus rises, –
here lest weeds choke off a fat harvest, elsewhere
lest the scant moisture desert the barren sand.   70

By turns let planted land lie fallow after reaping
and let the idle field crust over with neglect.
Or, beneath the next star sow golden spelt
where late you gleaned the bright bean in its trembling
pod, the blooms of slender vetch, or the bitter
lupine with frail stem and whispering leaves. Indeed,
a crop of flax will parch a field, and oats will parch,
and poppies dewed with Lethean slumber parch.
But crop rotation is easy work – only do not blush
to lave the parched acres with luxuriant dung   80
nor to scatter grimy ashes over the exhausted ground.
Changing crops this way gives the soil rest
without the parsimony of unplanted earth.
Then, too, it often pays to torch sterile fields,
and to scorch with crackling flame the wisps of stubble,
whether soil draws strength unseen and rich sustenance
from fire, or that by flame corruption's pasteurized away
and worthless damp sweats out, or that heat opens up
fresh vesicles and loosens obscured pores
through which sap might come to tender shoots, or rather
     that it kilns   90
the clay and constricts gaping veins, so that no fine
drizzle, nor the sun's ravishing force, nor
the northwind's piercing chill may blast the sprouts.
He helps his land who breaks down scurf with a mattock
and drags the willow-switch harrow – not for nothing
does golden Ceres smile on him from high Olympus! –

et qui, proscisso quae suscitat aequore terga,
rursus in obliquum verso perrumpit aratro,
exercetque frequens tellurem atque imperat arvis.

100   Umida solstitia atque hiemes orate serenas,
agricolae: hiberno laetissima pulvere farra,
laetus ager; nullo tantum se Mysia cultu
iactat et ipsa suas mirantur Gargara messis.
quid dicam, iacto qui semine comminus arva
insequitur cumulosque ruit male pinguis harenae
deinde satis fluvium inducit rivosque sequentis
et, cum exustus ager morientibus aestuat herbis,
ecce supercilio clivosi tramitis undam
elicit? illa cadens raucum per levia murmur
110   saxa ciet scatebrisque arentia temperat arva.
quid qui, ne gravidis procumbat culmus aristis,
luxuriem segetum tenera depascit in herba,
cum primum sulcos aequant sata? quique paludis
collectum umorem bibula deducit harena?
praesertim incertis si mensibus amnis abundans
exit et obducto late tenet omnia limo,
unde cavae tepido sudant umore lacunae.

Nec tamen, haec cum sint hominumque boumque labores
versando terram experti, nihil inprobus anser
120   Strymoniaeque grues et amaris intiba fibris
officiunt aut umbra nocet. pater ipse colendi
haud facilem esse viam voluit, primusque per artem
movit agros, curis acuens mortalia corda,
nec torpere gravi passus sua regna veterno.
ante Iovem nulli subigebant arva coloni;
ne signare quidem aut partiri limite campum
fas erat: in medium quaerebant, ipsaque tellus
omnia liberius nullo poscente ferebat.
ille malum virus serpentibus addidit atris,

and he who having harrowed up his plain to ridges
turns to plough crosswise through what he raised.
He ever disciplines his earth, commands his tilth.

For humid summers and winters mild, pray,   100
O farmers: wheat delights in winter's dust,
our field is flush – no tillage makes Mysia flaunt
as richly, and Gargara's agape at her own harvests.
Why mention him who, having cast his seeds,
grapples hand to soil and razes fruitless sandheaps,
then leads in the stream and its eddying ripples?
When the heatstruck field swelters, shoots withering,
look! – from a hillcrest ditch he taps a runlet
which falling sounds a low racket through sleek stones
and with its gushing slakes the thirsty earth.   110
And what of him who, lest stalks droop with corpulent
        ears,
mows the rampant grain in its green delicacy
when first the crop grows even with the furrow?
Or him who drains the marsh's hoard of water
into the sumping absorbency of sand, especially if
in capricious months the swollen river floods
and swathes the wide scape in a skin of silt,
so that the land's hollows seep with warm droplets?

And yet, though seasoned men and oxen struggle thus
to turn the soil, still the fractious gander spoils their work,
or Thracian cranes, or bitter-leaved chicory,   120
or shade harms the crops. The Father himself willed the
        way
of husbandry to be severe, first stirred by ingenuity
the fields, honing mortal skill with tribulation,
and suffered not his realm to laze in lumpish sloth.
Before Jove no yeoman groomed the soil: to mark
the ground or to divide with fences was sacrilege.
In fellowship men strove, and the earth herself,
unpestered, more freely fruited her abundance.
But he put dire venom into vipers black, bade wolves

130   praedarique lupos iussit pontumque moveri,
       mellaque decussit foliis, ignemque removit,
       et passim rivis currentia vina repressit,
       ut varias usus meditando extunderet artis
       paulatim et sulcis frumenti quaereret herbam,
       et silicis venis abstrusum excuderet ignem.
       tunc alnos primum fluvii sensere cavatas;
       navita tum stellis numeros et nomina fecit,
       Pleiadas, Hyadas, claramque Lycaonis Arcton;
       tum laqueis captare feras et fallere visco
140   inventum et magnos canibus circumdare saltus;
       atque alius latum funda iam verberat amnem
       alta petens, pelagoque alius trahit umida lina;
       tum ferri rigor atque argutae lamina serrae
       (nam primi cuneis scindebant fissile lignum),
       tum variae venere artes. labor omnia vicit
       improbus et duris urgens in rebus egestas.

       Prima Ceres ferro mortalis vertere terram
       instituit, cum iam glandes atque arbuta sacrae
       deficerent silvae et victum Dodona negaret.
150   mox et frumentis labor additus, ut mala culmos
       esset robigo segnisque horreret in arvis
       carduus; intereunt segetes, subit aspera silva,
       lappaeque tribolique, interque nitentia culta
       infelix lolium et steriles dominantur avenae.
       quod nisi et adsiduis herbam insectabere rastris
       et sonitu terrebis aves et ruris opaci
       falce premes umbram votisque vocaveris imbrem,
       heu magnum alterius frustra spectabis acervum
       concussaque famem in silvis solabere quercu.

                              *

to raven and the sea to heave, shook honey from the leaves,130
secreted fire, stanched the wine that ran everywhere in
     streams,
so that need with contemplation might forge sundry arts
in time, might seek in furrows the blade of wheat
and strike from flinty veins the hidden spark.
Then first did rivers heft the hollowed alder,
then the sailor plotted out the stars, numbering and
     naming:
Pleiades, Hyades, and radiant, royal Arctos.
Then . . . . what discovery! – how to catch game in snares, to
     dupe
with birdlime, to encircle great woods with hounds.   140
Now one whips a wide river with a dragnet, probing
the depths, and one through the sea trawls his wet gear.
Then came hard iron, and the shrill sawblade
(for earliest men with wedges split the splintered timber),
and then myriad arts. Toil subdued the earth,
relentless toil, and the prick of dearth in hardship.

Ceres first taught men to turn the earth with iron
when arbutes and acorns dwindled in the sacred grove
and Dodona withheld her provender. But soon trouble
     grew
with crops, as mildew's blight devoured the stalks   150
and lazy thistles bristled in the fields: grain fails, a scraggly
     wood
springs up with burrs and caltrops, and among the
     bronzing acres
the contrary tares and feckless reed are despots.
If you harry not with tireless rake the weeds,
if with your voice you do not terrify the birds
or with your sickle prune the canopy shading the land,
if with no prayers you call down rain,
O! how you'll gaze in vain at another's ample stockpile
and shake the forest oak to soothe your famine.

*

160 Dicendum et quae sint duris agrestibus arma,
      quis sine nec potuere seri nec surgere messes:
      vomis et inflexi primum grave robur aratri,
      tardaque Eleusinae matris volventia plaustra,
      tribulaque traheaeque et iniquo pondere rastri;
      virgea praeterea Celei vilisque supellex,
      arbuteae crates et mystica vannus Iacchi.
      omnia quae multo ante memor provisa repones,
      si te digna manet divini gloria ruris.
      continuo in silvis magna vi flexa domatur
170 in burim et curvi formam accipit ulmus aratri.
      huic a stirpe pedes temo protentus in octo,
      binae aures, duplici aptantur dentalia dorso.
      caeditur et tilia ante iugo levis altaque fagus
      stivaque, quae currus a tergo torqueat imos,
      et suspensa focis explorat robora fumus.

      Possum multa tibi veterum praecepta referre,
      ni refugis tenuisque piget cognoscere curas.

      Area cum primis ingenti aequanda cylindro
      et vertenda manu et creta solidanda tenaci,
180 ne subeant herbae neu pulvere victa fatiscat,
      tum variae inludant pestes: saepe exiguus mus
      sub terris posuitque domos atque horrea fecit,
      aut oculis capti fodere cubilia talpae,
      inventusque cavis bufo et quae plurima terrae
      monstra ferunt, populatque ingentem farris acervum
      curculio atque inopi metuens formica senectae.

      Contemplator item, cum se nux plurima silvis
      induet in florem et ramos curvabit olentis.
      si superant fetus, pariter frumenta sequentur
190 magnaque cum magno veniet tritura calore;

I must describe the brawny farmer's arsenal,   160
without which crops are neither sown nor grown.
First the share and heavy hardwood of the curving plough,
the slow-trundling wagons of Ceres, threshers and sledges,
hoes brutally heavy, and more – simple wicker goods from
   Eleusis:
berry crates, the winnowing-fan of bacchant sanctity . . .
All these remember, plan for, lay in long beforehand
if the land's sublime glory is justly to await you.
From first growth in the forest, the elm bent by long force
is trained for the stock, and learns the shape of the
   plough's curve.   170
To its shaft is fixed an eight-foot pole with two
   mouldboards
and a split-backed plough-beam. Beforehand cut light
   linden
for the yoke, and for the grip a length of beech
to steer the contraption's chassis from rearward,
and hang the timber hearthside for smoke to season.

I can recite you precepts old and many
if you don't bolt, loath to master 'trifles'.

The threshing-floor must first be levelled by a massive
   roller,
riled by hand, concreted with tenacious clay,
lest weeds slip in or, crumbling to dust, it gap   180
and teeming pests mock you. Often the tiny mouse
homesteads underground and installs his granaries,
or blind moles burrow chambers. In hollows
find the toad and what legion monsters the earth whelps.
The weevil plunders a huge heap of grain – or the ant,
dreading an impoverished age.

Take note when in the woods many a walnut tree
pranks herself in blossom, droops her fragrant branches.
If nuts flourish, grain will follow,
and great threshing come with great heats.   190

at si luxuria foliorum exuberat umbra,
nequiquam pinguis palea teret area culmos.
semina vidi equidem multos medicare serentis
et nitro prius et nigra perfundere amurca,
grandior ut fetus siliquis fallacibus esset,
et, quamvis igni exiguo, properata maderent.
vidi lecta diu et multo spectata labore
degenerare tamen, ni vis humana quotannis
maxima quaeque manu legeret. sic omnia fatis
200   in peius ruere ac retro sublapsa referri,
non aliter, quam qui adverso vix flumine lembum
remigiis subigit, si bracchia forte remisit,
atque illum in praeceps prono rapit alveus amni.

Praeterea tam sunt Arcturi sidera nobis
Haedorumque dies servandi et lucidus Anguis,
quam quibus in patriam ventosa per aequora vectis
Pontus et ostriferi fauces temptantur Abydi.
Libra die somnique pares ubi fecerit horas
et medium luci atque umbris iam dividit orbem,
210   exercete, viri, tauros, serite hordea campis
usque sub extremum brumae intractabilis imbrem;
nec non et lini segetem et Cereale papaver
tempus humo tegere et iamdudum incumbere aratris,
dum sicca tellure licet, dum nubila pendent.
vere fabis satio; tum te quoque, Medica, putres
accipiunt sulci et milio venit annua cura,
candidus auratis aperit cum cornibus annum
Taurus et adverso cedens Canis occidit astro.
at si triticeam in messem robustaque farra
220   exercebis humum solisque instabis aristis,
ante tibi Eoae Atlantides abscondantur
Cnosiaque ardentis decedat stella Coronae,
debita quam sulcis committas semina quamque
invitae properes anni spem credere terrae.

But if shade thrives, an extravagance of leaves,
for naught your threshing-floor will thresh stalks thick with
    chaff.
I've known many sowers to minister to seeds,
to sprinkle with saltpetre, steep in black oil-dregs,
that beans might plump within the pod's deceptive bulk,
and, though the fire be small, hastily stew.
I've seen seeds long chosen and attended with much labour
still degenerate if human sinew culled not
the fattest out by hand each year. So by decree
all things incline to worse, and foundering backslide, back   200
like one whose oar can scarcely thrust his skiff upstream;
if perchance he slack his arms, sternward
the coursing water drags him down the rapids.

Now. We must watch the stars – Arcturus,
the bright Snake, the days of the Kids –
as they do who homebound sail on squalling seas,
braving the Pontus and the oystered maw of Abydos.
When Libra balances the hours of day and sleep
and parts the world in halves of light and shade,
men, exercise your oxen, sow your fields with barley   210
right to the edge of winter's rain, too wild to work.
Then's time to bury flaxseed in earth, and the poppy
of Ceres, and well past time to lean into the plough
while the dry soil allows it, while yet the gloom hangs
    back.
Spring's for planting beans; then too the ripe furrows
    welcome
alfalfa, and millet comes into our annual vigilance
as the dazzling Bull with gilded horns opens the year
and the Dog Star sets, shrinking from his starry foe.
But if for wheaten harvest and hardy spelt
you ready your ground, if you're after grain alone,   220
let first at dawn the Pleiades drop from sight
and the blazing Crown's sovereign star withdraw
before you remit to furrows your debt of seeds
or rush to trust a year's hope to reluctant dirt.

multi ante occasum Maiae coepere; sed illos
exspectata seges vanis elusit avenis.
si vero viciamque seres vilemque phaselum,
nec Pelusiacae curam aspernabere lentis,
haud obscura cadens mittet tibi signa Bootes:
230 incipe et ad medias sementem extende pruinas.

Idcirco certis dimensum partibus orbem
per duodena regit mundi sol aureus astra.
quinque tenent caelum zonae; quarum una corusco
semper sole rubens et torrida semper ab igni;
quam circum extremae dextra laevaque trahuntur
caeruleae, glacie concretae atque imbribus atris;
has inter mediamque duae mortalibus aegris
munere concessae divum, et via secta per ambas,
obliquus qua se signorum verteret ordo.
240 mundus ut ad Scythiam Rhipaeasque arduus arces
consurgit, premitur Libyae devexus in Austros.
hic vertex nobis semper sublimis; at illum
sub pedibus Styx atra videt Manesque profundi.
maximus hic flexu sinuoso elabitur Anguis
circum perque duas in morem fluminis Arctos,
Arctos Oceani metuentis aequore tingui.
illic, ut perhibent, aut intempesta silet nox,
semper et obtenta densentur nocte tenebrae;
aut redit a nobis Aurora diemque reducit,
250 nosque ubi primus equis Oriens adflavit anhelis,
illic sera rubens accendit lumina Vesper.
hinc tempestates dubio praediscere caelo
possumus, hinc messisque diem tempusque serendi,
et quando infidum remis impellere marmor
conveniat, quando armatas deducere classis,
aut tempestivam silvis evertere pinum.
nec frustra signorum obitus speculamur et ortus,
temporibusque parem diversis quattuor annum.

*

Many begin before Maia sets westward, but
their looked-for crop chaffs with empty husks.
But if you sow the vetch or common eye-bean,
and do not scorn the care of Nile lentils, never
will westing Boötes blazon forth a dim signal.
Snap to, and keep seeding till midwinter's frosts.   230

For this the golden sun maintains its orbit
marked through the zodiacal twelve in marches fixed.
Five zones comprise the firmament, of which one ever
    blushes
under the flaring sun, ever scorched by its fire.
Around this at the poles to right and left stretch
bleak zones, ice-crusted and dark with storms.
Between the ice and middle fire, two zones to frail
    humanity
by grace of God are granted. A path cuts through them both
on which oblique the ranks of constellations spin.
As the earth surges steeply up to Scythia   240
and the Rhipean crags, so it sinks sloping to Libya's south.
The zenith ever vaults above us, the nadir
underfoot glowers at inky Styx and shades infernal.
Vast with sinuous coils here glides the Serpent,
weaving like a river round and through the Bears –
two Bears that fear to plunge the ocean's plane.
There, they say, may lurk dank night
and the shadows ever clotting under night's shroud . . .
or else Dawn removes from us, returns their day
and when sunrise with his panting team first breathes   250
on us, there ruddy Vesper kindles the late hour's lights.
So we can forecast weather though the sky
equivocate, so know the harvest-day, the time to sow,
when to smack with oars the sea's treacherous slate
and when to launch the bristling fleet
or in the woods to topple the ready pine.
Not in vain do we observe the rise and set of signs
and the year, orderly in its four dissimilar seasons.

*

Frigidus agricolam si quando continet imber,
260   multa, forent quae mox caelo properanda sereno,
maturare datur: durum procudit arator
vomeris obtunsi dentem, cavat arbore lintres,
aut pecori signum aut numeros impressit acervis.
exacuunt alii vallos furcasque bicornis
atque Amerina parant lentae retinacula viti.
nunc facilis rubea texatur fiscina virga,
nunc torrete igni fruges, nunc frangite saxo.
quippe etiam festis quaedam exercere diebus
fas et iura sinunt: rivos deducere nulla
270   religio vetuit, segeti praetendere saepem,
insidias avibus moliri, incendere vepres,
balantumque gregem fluvio mersare salubri.
saepe oleo tardi costas agitator aselli
vilibus aut onerat pomis, lapidemque revertens
incusum aut atrae massam picis urbe reportat.

Ipsa dies alios alio dedit ordine Luna
felicis operum. quintam fuge: pallidus Orcus
Eumenidesque satae; tum partu Terra nefando
Coeumque Iapetumque creat saevumque Typhoea
280   et coniuratos caelum rescindere fratres.
ter sunt conati imponere Pelio Ossam
scilicet, atque Ossae frondosum involvere Olympum;
ter pater exstructos disiecit fulmine montis.
septima post decimam felix et ponere vitem
et prensos domitare boves et licia telae
addere. nona fugae melior, contraria furtis.

Multa adeo gelida melius se nocte dedere,
aut cum sole novo terras inrorat Eous.
nocte leves melius stipulae, nocte arida prata
290   tondentur, noctes lentus non deficit umor.
et quidam seros hiberni ad luminis ignis
pervigilat ferroque faces inspicat acuto;
interea longum cantu solata laborem

Whenever chill sleet coops the farmer up,
he can accomplish much that under a cloudless sky   260
he'd rush: the ploughman tools the blunted share's
rough teeth, scoops troughs from tree-trunks,
brands his seal on livestock or reckons up his ricks.
Some whittle pales to point, or two-pronged props,
or fashion willow-cords to hold the lithe vine.
Now weave the lenient basket from bramble switches.
Now fire-roast grain, now grind beneath the millstone.
Even on holy-days, civic laws and sacred
allow some labour. To guide the irrigation ditch down
no reverence forbids, to screen crops with hedgerows,   270
build birdtraps, torch briars, dip sheep in the creek's tonic.
The muleteer often loads his mule's slow flanks
with oil or cheap fruits, and returning from town
hauls a grooved millstone, or a black lump of pitch.

Distinct days with distinct phases the Moon herself
has consecrated auspicious for work. Avoid
the fifth: then Earth spawned forth pale Orcus
and the Furies, and Coeus and Iapetus
and in travail abhorrent raging Typhoeus,
and those brothers who conspired to tear down heaven.   280
Thrice they ventured to pile Ossa onto Pelion –
it's true! – and roll tree-lined Olympus onto Ossa.
Thrice the Father's lightning wrecked their cobbled-up
     summit.
The seventeenth bodes well for setting vines,
for breaking cows corralled and threading the loom.
The ninth abets the runaway, but thwarts intrigues.

Many tasks lend themselves better to cool night,
or when at dawn the morning star dews the earth.
At night fine stubble, at night dry meadows are best mown,
night never lacks the retting damp.   290
One man before the late flame of a winter lamp
lingers wakeful, and with his axe's edge tapers torchpoles
while, consoling her long toil with song,

arguto coniunx percurrit pectine telas,
aut dulcis musti Volcano decoquit umorem
et foliis undam trepidi despumat aëni.
at rubicunda Ceres medio succiditur aestu,
et medio tostas aestu terit area fruges.
nudus ara, sere nudus; hiems ignava colono.
300 frigoribus parto agricolae plerumque fruuntur
mutuaque inter se laeti convivia curant.
invitat genialis hiems curasque resolvit,
ceu pressae cum iam portum tetigere carinae,
puppibus et laeti nautae imposuere coronas.
sed tamen et quernas glandes tum stringere tempus
et lauri bacas oleamque cruentaque myrta,
tum gruibus pedicas et retia ponere cervis
auritosque sequi lepores, tum figere dammas
stuppea torquentem Balearis verbera fundae,
310 cum nix alta iacet, glaciem cum flumina trudunt.

Quid tempestates autumni et sidera dicam,
atque, ubi iam breviorque dies et mollior aestas,
quae vigilanda viris, vel cum ruit imbriferum ver,
spicea iam campis cum messis inhorruit et cum
frumenta in viridi stipula lactentia turgent?
saepe ego, cum flavis messorem induceret arvis
agricola et fragili iam stringeret hordea culmo,
omnia ventorum concurrere proelia vidi,
quae gravidam late segetem ab radicibus imis
320 sublimem expulsam eruerent; ita turbine nigro
ferret hiems culmumque levem stipulasque volantis.
saepe etiam inmensum caelo venit agmen aquarum
et foedam glomerant tempestatem imbribus atris
collectae ex alto nubes; ruit arduus aether,
et pluvia ingenti sata laeta boumque labores
diluit; implentur fossae et cava flumina crescunt
cum sonitu fervetque fretis spirantibus aequor.
ipse pater media nimborum in nocte corusca
fulmina molitur dextra, quo maxima motu

his wife with shrill shuttle zips across the warp
or at the hearth reduces the grape's sweet juices,
skimming off the pot's rolling current with a frond.
But auburn grain is reaped in heat of noon,
in heat of noon the threshing-floor flails the husks:
strip to plough, strip to sow. Winter is the farmer's
    breather.
In cold snaps farmers revel in their yield   300
and treat themselves to mutual banqueting with pleasure.
Winter's gaity stirs them, melts their cares,
as when at last the laden keels make port
and giddy sailors drape the decks in garlands.
Still, now's time to pluck acorns and bayberries,
olives and the fruit of the blood-red myrtle,
time to lay snares for cranes and nets for deer,
to track the long-eared hare, time to knock down the doe,
to whirl the hempen thongs of your Balearic sling,
when snow lies deep, when rivers shove through ice.   310

Why tell of autumn's storms and stars
and, now days draw in and summer softens, what keeps
men to vigil? – now or when spring falls in downpours
as the sheathed harvest needles through the field
and grain on its green stem swells up with milk?
Often, as the farmer guides the reaper to his golden tract
and shears the barley from its crackling stalk,
I have seen all the armies of wind clash
uprooting plump grain left and right from deepest roots
and hurling it high, then with its whirlwind black   320
the storm whisks the slight straw and airborne slips away.
And often in the sky looms a tremendous host of waters –
clouds levied from the ether roll a murky squall
of swart rains: shelved heaven tumbles, and with its wet
pounding washes off the lilting crop, the oxen's labours.
The gutters fill, the gully swells with rushing,
the sea seethes, its estuaries heaving.
The Father himself, in his midnight of clouds, hurls
with his fulgent fist the thunderbolt, at whose impact

330   terra tremit: fugere ferae et mortalia corda
       per gentis humilis stravit pavor; ille flagranti
       aut Athon aut Rhodopen aut alta Ceraunia telo
       deicit; ingeminant Austri et densissimus imber;
       nunc nemora ingenti vento, nunc litora plangunt.

       Hoc metuens caeli menses et sidera serva,
       frigida Saturni sese quo stella receptet,
       quos ignis caelo Cyllenius erret in orbis.
       in primis venerare deos, atque annua magnae
       sacra refer Cereri laetis operatus in herbis
340   extremae sub casum hiemis, iam vere sereno.
       tum pingues agni et tum mollissima vina,
       tum somni dulces densaeque in montibus umbrae.
       cuncta tibi Cererem pubes agrestis adoret:
       cui tu lacte favos et miti dilue Baccho,
       terque novas circum felix eat hostia fruges,
       omnis quam chorus et socii comitentur ovantes,
       et Cererem clamore vocent in tecta; neque ante
       falcem maturis quisquam supponat aristis
       quam Cereri torta redimitus tempora quercu
350   det motus incompositos et carmina dicat.

       Atque haec ut certis possemus discere signis,
       aestusque pluviasque et agentis frigora ventos,
       ipse pater statuit, quid menstrua luna moneret,
       quo signo caderent Austri, quid saepe videntes
       agricolae propius stabulis armenta tenerent.
       continuo ventis surgentibus aut freta ponti
       incipiunt agitata tumescere et aridus altis
       montibus audiri fragor, aut resonantia longe
       litora misceri et nemorum increbrescere murmur.
360   iam sibi tum a curvis male temperat unda carinis,

the earth's bulk trembles: critters scatter, terror blasts   330
all mortal hearts to cowering. He with lancing fire
sunders Athos or Rhodope or the heights of Ceraunia.
The southwind redoubles, and the thronging rain.
Now thickets, now shores moan beneath the savage gale.

Fearing this, observe the months and heaven's
          constellations –
where Saturn's frozen star runs retrograde,
into which of heaven's orbits wanders Mercury with his
          fires.
Above all, love the gods, and to exalted Ceres
devote your yearly tribute, performed on the reviving grass
as the last of winter falters, at the crack of clement spring.   340
Then lambs are fat and wine is mellow,
then sleep is sweet as shadows cluster on the peaks.
Let every farmhand worship Ceres: for her
infuse the honeycombs with milk and well-aged wine,
and thrice around the sprouts parade the blessed sacrifice
whom the chorus of your company trails with cordant
          jubilation,
with cheers invoking Ceres to dwell beneath their eaves.
Nor should any edge his sickle under the ripe ears
before he wreathes his brows with sprigs of oak,
spins an artless shuffle, and lifts his harvest hymn.   350

That by sure signs we may anticipate
these heats and torrents, the wind that speeds the ice,
the Father himself ordained the monthly omens of the
          moon,
at what sign the southwinds fall, at what steady sightings
the farmer keeps his cattle near the stalls.
Always under gusting winds the salty straits
begin to churn and swell and dry thunder sounds
against the mountaintops, or shores resound
a tumult to the distances and the woodland murmur
          amplifies.
Then the tide restrains not from the curved keel,   360

cum medio celeres revolant ex aequore mergi
clamoremque ferunt ad litora, cumque marinae
in sicco ludunt fulicae, notasque paludes
deserit atque altam supra volat ardea nubem.
saepe etiam stellas vento inpendente videbis
praecipitis caelo labi, noctisque per umbram
flammarum longos a tergo albescere tractus;
saepe levem paleam et frondes volitare caducas
aut summa nantis in aqua colludere plumas.

370   at Boreae de parte trucis cum fulminat et cum
Eurique Zephyrique tonat domus, omnia plenis
rura natant fossis atque omnis navita ponto
umida vela legit. numquam inprudentibus imber
obfuit: aut illum surgentem vallibus imis
aëriae fugere grues, aut bucula caelum
suspiciens patulis captavit naribus auras,
aut arguta lacus circumvolitavit hirundo
et veterem in limo ranae cecinere querelam.
saepius et tectis penetralibus extulit ova
380   angustum formica terens iter, et bibit ingens
arcus, et e pastu decedens agmine magno
corvorum increpuit densis exercitus alis.
iam variae pelagi volucres et quae Asia circum
dulcibus in stagnis rimantur prata Caystri;
certatim largos umeris infundere rores,
nunc caput obiectare fretis, nunc currere in undas
et studio incassum videas gestire lavandi.
tum cornix plena pluviam vocat improba voce
et sola in sicca secum spatiatur harena.
390   ne nocturna quidem carpentes pensa puellae
nescivere hiemem, testa cum ardente viderent
scintillare oleum et putris concrescere fungos.

Nec minus ex imbri soles et aperta serena
prospicere et certis poteris cognoscere signis:
nam neque tum stellis acies obtunsa videtur,

when fleet the terns wheel shoreward from mid-ocean
shrieking to the strand, when sea-coots
frolic on dry land, and the heron quits her wonted swamps
to wing above the towering cloud.
Often, when wind freshens, you'll see stars
falling headlong down the sky, through the shades of night
trailing lengths of blanching flame behind.
Often too you'll see fine chaff and fallen leaves fluttering,
or on the water's surface feathers trifling as they skim.
But when from the grim northland levin flares, when   370
the mansions of the east- and westwind roll thunder,
the countryside entire sloshes under flooding ditches,
and every sea-bound sailor furls his soaked sails.
Never has rain worked ill unwarned: either as it masses
the aerial cranes dive for valleys deep, or the heifer
eyeing heaven tracks the breeze with flaring nostrils,
or the twitting swallow flits around the cisterns
and in the mire frogs croak their immemorial complaint.
More often, from her cloistered crannies the ant drags out
her eggs, wearing a threadlike groove, and a vaulting
     rainbow   380
stretches down to drink, and from the pasture departing
in grand array a raven army drums with frequent wings.
Already seabirds variegated, already birds like those
that comb the Asian lees around Cayster's comely
     oxbows –
see them vie to douse their shoulders in the heavy spray,
now thrusting heads under the stream, now rushing waves,
aimlessly dithered with zeal for bathing.
Then unruly the crow cries down rain with sharp tones
and solitary strolls the thirsty strand.
Even girls engrossed in nightly chores are never unaware   390
of brewing storms – they mark when in sparking lamps
the oil-light flickers and smutty mould collects.

After the rain, you can predict the sun and open skies
with no less foresight, and know their portents sure:
for then we view the stars' clean edges unblunted,

nec fratris radiis obnoxia surgere Luna,
tenuia nec lanae per caelum vellera ferri;
non tepidum ad solem pinnas in litore pandunt
dilectae Thetidi alcyones, non ore solutos
400   immundi meminere sues iactare maniplos.
at nebulae magis ima petunt campoque recumbunt,
solis et occasum servans de culmine summo
nequiquam seros exercet noctua cantus.
apparet liquido sublimis in aëre Nisus
et pro purpureo poenas dat Scylla capillo:
quacumque illa levem fugiens secat aethera pinnis,
ecce inimicus, atrox, magno stridore per auras
insequitur Nisus; qua se fert Nisus ad auras,
illa levem fugiens raptim secat aethera pinnis.
410   tum liquidas corvi presso ter gutture voces
aut quater ingeminant, et saepe cubilibus altis
nescio qua praeter solitum dulcedine laeti
inter se in foliis strepitant; iuvat imbribus actis
progeniem parvam dulcisque revisere nidos;
haud equidem credo, quia sit divinitus illis
ingenium aut rerum Fato prudentia maior;
verum ubi tempestas et caeli mobilis umor
mutavere vias et Iuppiter uvidus Austris
denset erant quae rara modo, et quae densa relaxat,
420   vertuntur species animorum, et pectora motus
nunc alios, alios dum nubila ventus agebat,
concipiunt: hinc ille avium concentus in agris
et laetae pecudes et ovantes gutture corvi.

Si vero solem ad rapidum lunasque sequentis
ordine respicies, numquam te crastina fallet
hora neque insidiis noctis capiere serenae.
luna revertentis cum primum colligit ignis,
si nigrum obscuro comprenderit aëra cornu,
maximus agricolis pelagoque parabitur imber;
430   at si virgineum suffuderit ore ruborem,

the Moon uprises as if not vassal to her brother's beams,
no cloud draws flimsy wool across the sky.
The halcyons dear to Thetis need not beach
and splay their feathers to catch the warm sun,
nor do the filthy hogs think to root and toss   400
the haybales with their snouts. But mists
probe vales and settle over fields, and gazing
on the setting sun from the rooftree's height
the owl rehearses her bootless evensong.
Ospreyed Nisus appears aloft in liquid air
and for his damson tress deals Scylla retribution:
where swerving she slashes the delicate air with wings,
there hostile, ruthless, screaming through the ether
Nisus follows; where Nisus towers through the ether,
swiftly swerving she slashes the delicate air with wings.
Then with tight gullets the crows re-echo three times   410
or four their strident cries, and high in their nests
blithe with a pleasure unaccustomed and strange
they chatter in the leaves. How glad, the rains disbanded,
to see again their tiny nestlings, their sweet thatch!
They've not, I think, some godsent native genius
or an extra share of prescience from the Fates,
but when the weather and erratic humours of the sky
shift course, when Jove, wet from the south,
condenses what was late dispersed, disperses
what was dense, the fancies of their minds are turned,   420
their breasts catch urges new, urges other
than when gales pursued the clouds. Hence that concert
of birds in the fields, hence the cattle's contentment,
the throaty raptures of the crows.

But if you mind the full-blast sun, the moons
succeeding in their order, never will the morrow's date
mislead you, nor the luring ambush of a cloudless night.
When first the moon gathers her returning fires,
if she clasps in dusky arms a hazy dark,
a heavy downpour primes for the ploughman and the surf.
If she overspreads her cheeks with virginal blushes   430

ventus erit; vento semper rubet aurea Phoebe.
sin ortu quarto (namque is certissimus auctor)
pura neque obtunsis per caelum cornibus ibit,
totus et ille dies et qui nascentur ab illo
exactum ad mensem pluvia ventisque carebunt,
votaque servati solvent in litore nautae
Glauco et Panopeae et Inoo Melicertae.

Sol quoque et exoriens et cum se condet in undas
signa dabit; solem certissima signa sequuntur,
et quae mane refert et quae surgentibus astris.
ille ubi nascentem maculis variaverit ortum
conditus in nubem medioque refugerit orbe,
suspecti tibi sint imbres; namque urget ab alto
arboribusque satisque Notus pecorique sinister.
aut ubi sub lucem densa inter nubila sese
diversi rumpent radii, aut ubi pallida surget
Tithoni croceum linquens Aurora cubile,
heu! male tum mitis defendet pampinus uvas:
tam multa in tectis crepitans salit horrida grando.
hoc etiam, emenso cum iam decedit Olympo,
profuerit meminisse magis; nam saepe videmus
ipsius in voltu varios errare colores:
caeruleus pluviam denuntiat, igneus Euros;
sin maculae incipient rutilo inmiscerier igni,
omnia tum pariter vento nimbisque videbis
fervere. non illa quisquam me nocte per altum
ire neque a terra moneat convellere funem.
at si, cum referetque diem condetque relatum,
lucidus orbis erit, frustra terrebere nimbis
et claro silvas cernes Aquilone moveri.

*

it will be wind – in wind the moon's gold always blushes.
But if at her fourth rising (for here's the surest token)
clear with horns unblurred she treads the sky,
that day entire and days that bloom therefrom
until the month's accomplished will laugh off winds and
    rain.
The mariners, safe ashore, tender their devotions
to Glaucus, Panope and Melicertes Ino's son.

The sun too, mounting east and plunging to the waves,
will offer signs: faithful signs attend the sun,
both reviving with the dawn and springing up with stars.   440
When wrapped in cloud and fled to his sphere's core
he streaks the early east with dappling,
watch out for rain, for from the heights bears down
the southwind, ruinous to copses, seedlings, and to flocks.
Or at first light, when through a cloudbank dense
scattered burst the sunbeams, or when Aurora pales to rise
leaving Tithonus' saffron bed – O! then how ill will
    grapeleaves
shield the tender clusters, so thickly bounce
the grainy hailstones banging on the rooftiles.
And this again will serve you to review: 450
when having scaled across Olympus the sun sinks
    westward,
often we observe upon his face transient hues
to waver: a livid one spells rain, fiery means eastwinds,
but if mottle starts to tinge with embered red,
then you'll see a fury everywhere of clouds and winds
    together.
On such a night let none induce me sail the deep
nor yank from land my mooring line.
But if, restoring day or stowing down the day restored,
lucent be his disk, pure folly to fear clouds,
and in a clear northwind you'll see the forests reel.   460

*

Denique, quid vesper serus vehat, unde serenas
ventus agat nubes, quid cogitet umidus Auster,
sol tibi signa dabit. solem quis dicere falsum
audeat? ille etiam caecos instare tumultus
saepe monet fraudemque et operta tumescere bella.
ille etiam exstincto miseratus Caesare Romam,
cum caput obscura nitidum ferrugine texit
impiaque aeternam timuerunt saecula noctem.
tempore quamquam illo tellus quoque et aequora ponti,
470   obscenaeque canes inportunaeque volucres
signa dabant. quotiens Cyclopum effervere in agros
vidimus undantem ruptis fornacibus Aetnam,
flammarumque globos liquefactaque volvere saxa!
armorum sonitum toto Germania caelo
audiit, insolitis tremuerunt motibus Alpes.
vox quoque per lucos volgo exaudita silentis
ingens, et simulacra modis pallentia miris
visa sub obscurum noctis, pecudesque locutae
(infandum!); sistunt amnes terraeque dehiscunt,
480   et maestum inlacrimat templis ebur aeraque sudant.
proluit insano contorquens vertice silvas
fluviorum rex Eridanus camposque per omnis
cum stabulis armenta tulit. nec tempore eodem
tristibus aut extis fibrae apparere minaces
aut puteis manare cruor cessavit, et altae
per noctem resonare lupis ululantibus urbes.
non alias caelo ceciderunt plura sereno
fulgura nec diri totiens arsere cometae.
ergo inter sese paribus concurrere telis
490   Romanas acies iterum videre Philippi;
nec fuit indignum superis, bis sanguine nostro
Emathiam et latos Haemi pinguescere campos.
scilicet et tempus veniet, cum finibus illis
agricola incurvo terram molitus aratro
exesa inveniet scabra robigine pila,

To nutshell: what the lingering dusk declares, whence
the wind drives sun-tipped clouds, what the sodden
    southwind
plots – of all, the sun will give you signs. Who dares
to call the sun a liar? It's often he who warns
that dark insurrection lurks, that perfidy and covert wars
    ferment.
It's he who, pitying Rome when Caesar's flame was
    snuffed,
shrouded his dazzling head with bloody gloom
and an impious generation feared eternal night.
But in that season the earth too, and the sea's expanse,
and baleful dogs, and troublous birds 470
gave signs. How often saw we over Sicilian fields
Aetna to boil, gushing forth from ruptured furnaces,
churning out globs of flame and molten rocks!
Germany heard the crash of arms throughout the sky.
The Alps shook with strange disturbances.
A voice sounded vastly through silent groves, and
sallow spectres of astonishing fashion sighted
under dim nightfall, and beasts – it is unspeakable –
took voice! Rivers halted, land rifted wide,
woeful the ivory wept in temples, and bronzes sweat. 480
Whirling in frenzied vortices, Eridanus king of rivers
swamped the forests, and through all the downs
swept herds away with their stables. Nor that season
did menacing fibrils cease to show in grim entrails
nor blood to run in wells, nor towered cities
through the night to echo with wolven howls.
Never dropped from fair sky more lightning
nor so often flared dire comets.
Thus Philippi again saw Roman troops
clash sword with fellow sword among themselves, 490
and heaven willed that twice Emathia and the wide
steppes of Thrace should glut upon our blood.
Surely time will come when in those fields
the farmer drudging soil with his curved plough
will turn up scabrous spears corroded by rust

aut gravibus rastris galeas pulsabit inanis
grandiaque effossis mirabitur ossa sepulchris.

Di patrii, Indigetes, et Romule Vestaque mater,
quae Tuscum Tiberim et Romana Palatia servas,
500   hunc saltem everso iuvenem succurrere saeclo
ne prohibete! satis iam pridem sanguine nostro
Laomedonteae luimus periuria Troiae;
iam pridem nobis caeli te regia, Caesar,
invidet atque hominum queritur curare triumphos;
quippe ubi fas versum atque nefas: tot bella per orbem,
tam multae scelerum facies; non ullus aratro
dignus honos, squalent abductis arva colonis
et curvae rigidum falces conflantur in ensem.
hinc movet Euphrates, illinc Germania bellum;
510   vicinae ruptis inter se legibus urbes
arma ferunt; saevit toto Mars impius orbe,
ut cum carceribus sese effudere quadrigae,
addunt in spatia, et frustra retinacula tendens
fertur equis auriga neque audit currus habenas.

or with his heavy hoe strike empty helmets,
and gape at massive bones in upturned graves.

Gods of my fathers, heroes of the land, Romulus
and mother Vesta, protectress of the Tuscan Tiber
and the regnant Roman hill, at least do not forbid   500
this noble stripling to succour a turvied age.
We've long ago atoned with ample blood
for Laomedon's perjury at Troy, and long the courts
of heaven have begrudged you here among us,
Caesar, grumbling that you overprize your mortal
    triumphs.
For good and ill have been transposed – so many wars
throughout the world! so massed the forms of sin!
No rightful honour to the plough; the croppers
    commandeered,
soil weeds to rot; and hooked sickles are forged to rigid
    swords.
Here Euphrates roils up war, there Germany.   510
Their mutual treaties shattered, neighboured
cities take up arms. The impious war-god savages the earth,
as when from the starting gate chariots surge
gaining speed lap by lap, and hauling vainly on the leathers
the teamster's hurtled onward by his horses, and the rig
    heeds not the reins.

Book Two

LIBER II

Hactenus arvorum cultus et sidera caeli:
nunc te, Bacche, canam, nec non silvestria tecum
virgulta et prolem tarde crescentis olivae.
huc, pater o Lenaee: tuis hic omnia plena
muneribus, tibi pampineo gravidus autumno
floret ager, spumat plenis vindemia labris;
huc, pater o Lenaee, veni nudataque musto
tingue novo mecum dereptis crura cothurnis.

Principio arboribus varia est natura creandis.
10 namque aliae nullis hominum cogentibus ipsae
sponte sua veniunt camposque et flumina late
curva tenent, ut molle siler lentaeque genestae,
populus et glauca canentia fronde salicta;
pars autem posito surgunt de semine, ut altae
castaneae, nemorumque Iovi quae maxima frondet
aesculus, atque habitae Grais oracula quercus.
pullulat ab radice aliis densissima silva,
ut cerasis ulmisque; etiam Parnasia laurus
parva sub ingenti matris se subicit umbra.
20 hos natura modos primum dedit, his genus omne
silvarum fruticumque viret nemorumque sacrorum.
sunt alii, quos ipse via sibi repperit usus.
hic plantas tenero abscindens de corpore matrum
deposuit sulcis, hic stirpes obruit arvo
quadrifidasque sudes et acuto robore vallos;
silvarumque aliae pressos propaginis arcus

BOOK TWO

Until now the care of crops and stars of heaven . . .
now you, O Bacchus, will I sing, and with you
forest shoots and the fruit of the slow-maturing olive.
Here, O winepress sire! Here abounds the fullness
of your bounties, here for you the ground blooms
burgeoning in vine-spread autumn, for you the vintage
froths in brimming vats – here, O winepress sire, come
tug your boots and dye bare legs with me in the new must!

First off, at propagating trees, nature is versatile.
For some with no man's coaxing volunteer,   10
sprouting themselves, taking the fields and flats
of winding rivers: the lissome willow and the hardy broom,
the poplar and pale osier-stands with silvered leaves.
Some spring from fallen seed: high chestnuts, the oak
that greens magnificent the Jovan groves
and the oak believed oracular by Greeks.
With others thickest shoots sprout out from the taproot,
as with cherries and with elms; the Delphic laurel
tiny beneath its mother's spacious shade thrusts up.
These methods nature first supplied, these foliate   20
the forest full of trees and shrubs, and the sacred woods.
Other techniques practice has gleaned along the way.
One man stripping suckers from the mother's tender trunk
set them in furrows, another planted stocks in soil,
and stakes split decussate, and pales of sharpened
        hardwood.
Some trees await the arch of layers bent low,

exspectant et viva sua plantaria terra;
nil radicis egent aliae summumque putator
haud dubitat terrae referens mandare cacumen.
30   quin et caudicibus sectis (mirabile dictu)
truditur e sicco radix oleagina ligno.
et saepe alterius ramos impune videmus
vertere in alterius, mutatamque insita mala
ferre pirum et prunis lapidosa rubescere corna.

Quare agite o proprios generatim discite cultus,
agricolae, fructusque feros mollite colendo,
neu segnes iaceant terrae. iuvat Ismara Baccho
conserere atque olea magnum vestire Taburnum.
tuque ades inceptumque una decurre laborem,
40   o decus, o famae merito pars maxima nostrae,
Maecenas, pelagoque volans da vela patenti.
non ego cuncta meis amplecti versibus opto,
non, mihi si linguae centum sint oraque centum,
ferrea vox. ades et primi lege litoris oram;
in manibus terrae. non hic te carmine ficto
atque per ambages et longa exorsa tenebo.

Sponte sua quae se tollunt in luminis oras,
infecunda quidem, sed laeta et fortia surgunt;
quippe solo natura subest. tamen haec quoque, si quis
50   inserat aut scrobibus mandet mutata subactis,
exuerint silvestrem animum, cultuque frequenti
in quascumque voles artis haud tarda sequentur.
nec non et sterilis quae stirpibus exit ab imis,
hoc faciat, vacuos si sit digesta per agros;
nunc altae frondes et rami matris opacant
crescentique adimunt fetus uruntque ferentem.
iam quae seminibus iactis se sustulit arbos
tarda venit seris factura nepotibus umbram,
pomaque degenerant sucos oblita priores,
60   et turpis avibus praedam fert uva racemos.

*

slips quickened in their own root-soil.
Others need no root: the pruner doesn't hesitate
to entrust the topmost cuttings to the earth.
Why, when its trunks are hewn – miraculous to tell! –   30
the olive pushes out a root from dry logs.
And often one tree's branches do we see benignly
turned into another's: transformed the pear hoists
grafted apples, and on the plum tree stony cornels blush.

Go then, orchardmen! – learn husbandry specific
to each species, the wild fruits taming by cultivation,
nor let your grounds lie idle. What delight to twine
Ismarus with vines, to dress great Taburnus with olives.
O come and ply with me this ventured task,
O my glory, O Maecenas, worthy of the best part of our
     fame,   40
spread open sails and wing for open sea!
I don't desire to comprehend the universe in my verse,
not if I had a hundred tongues, a hundred mouths,
an iron voice. O come and coast the headland's hem
hard by the shore: I will not keep you here
with inkhorn snarls or long preamble.

Trees that unforced lift themselves to realms of light
grow up fruitless but fair and strong;
their nature inheres in the soil, but even these
if grafted, or to toiled-up trenches' custody transplanted,   50
will shake their wildwood temper, and with constant
     cultivation
follow readily in what course you desire.
The shoot that barren breaks from the stalk's base
would likewise tame if spread through open land,
where now its mother's high boughs and bracts overshade
and deprive it fruited increase, vex its yield.
Again, the tree that rears itself from cast-off seeds
waxes slowly, a bowered gift to far posterity,
but its fruit degenerates, forgetting its old savour,
and the vine yields misbegotten clusters, plunder for birds.   60

*

Scilicet omnibus est labor impendendus et omnes
cogendae in sulcum ac multa mercede domandae.
sed truncis oleae melius, propagine vites
respondent, solido Paphiae de robore myrtus;
plantis edurae coryli nascuntur et ingens
fraxinus Herculeaeque arbos umbrosa coronae
Chaoniique patris glandes; etiam ardua palma
nascitur et casus abies visura marinos.
inseritur vero et fetu nucis arbutus horrida,
70   et steriles platani malos gessere valentis;
castaneae fagus, ornusque incanuit albo
flore piri, glandemque sues fregere sub ulmis.

Nec modus inserere atque oculos inponere simplex.
nam qua se medio trudunt de cortice gemmae
et tenuis rumpunt tunicas, angustus in ipso
fit nodo sinus: huc aliena ex arbore germen
includunt udoque docent inolescere libro.
aut rursum enodes trunci resecantur et alte
finditur in solidum cuneis via, deinde feraces
80   plantae immittuntur: nec longum tempus, et ingens
exiit ad caelum ramis felicibus arbos,
miraturque novas frondes et non sua poma.

Praeterea genus haud unum nec fortibus ulmis
nec salici lotoque neque Idaeis cyparissis,
nec pingues unam in faciem nascuntur olivae,
orchades et radii et amara pausia baca,
pomaque et Alcinoi silvae, nec surculus idem
Crustumiis Syriisque piris gravibusque volemis.
non eadem arboribus pendet vindemia nostris,
90   quam Methymnaeo carpit de palmite Lesbos;
sunt Thasiae vites, sunt et Mareotides albae,
pinguibus hae terris habiles, levioribus illae,
et passo Psithia utilior tenuisque Lageos
temptatura pedes olim vincturaque linguam,

To all, of course, apply your labours – all
arrayed in furrows and tamed at heavy cost.
But olive trees to truncheons, vines to layers
best respond, Cyprian myrtles to solid heartwood stakes.
From suckers sturdy hazels stem, and the spiring
ash, whose shadowing boughs crowned Hercules,
and the Father's Dodonan oaks; so the sheer palm too
uprises, and the fir that will see ocean perils.
Grafted the bristly arbute gets a walnut slip
and the barren plane-tree bears robust apples,   70
the beech whitens with the white of chestnut blossoms,
the ash whitens with pear, and pigs crunch acorns under
     elms.

Nor are the sciences of budding and grafting all one.
For where buds push themselves from bast
and burst their fragile calyces a narrow slit is made
smack on the node: here from an alien tree insert
a bud and train it up to thrive in the succulent xylem.
But in grafting, knotless stocks are split, and deep
an opening cleft with wedges to the pith, then fruitful
scions slipped in: not long and a huge tree   80
reaches skyward with branches flourishing,
amazed at its new leaves, fruits not its own.

Nor yet are the strains of sturdy elm unvaried,
nor of willows, lotus, cypresses of Ida.
Nor sprout balmed olives with a single show –
pausian olives are fat and bitter, the orchas oval, the radius
     long –
nor apples in Alcinous' orchards, nor are cuttings alike
of Syrian pears, Crustumian pears, the pears that heavy
fill the hand. On our grapetrees hangs a different vintage
than Lesbos plucks from Methymna's boughs: 90
there are Thasian vines, blond Mareotic vines
(these for rich soils fit, those for meagre),
the Psithian, best for raisin-wine, the subtle Lagean
sure to flout the legs and flummox the tongue,

purpureae preciaeque, et quo te carmine dicam,
Rhaetica? nec cellis ideo contende Falernis.
sunt et Aminneae vites, firmissima vina,
Tmolius adsurgit quibus et rex ipse Phanaeus;
Argitisque minor, cui non certaverit ulla
100 aut tantum fluere aut totidem durare per annos.
non ego te, dis et mensis accepta secundis,
transierim, Rhodia, et tumidis, Bumaste, racemis.
sed neque quam multae species nec nomina quae sint
est numerus, neque enim numero comprendere refert;
quem qui scire velit, Libyci velit aequoris idem
discere quam multae Zephyro turbentur harenae,
aut ubi navigiis violentior incidit Eurus,
nosse quot Ionii veniant ad litora fluctus.

Nec vero terrae ferre omnes omnia possunt.
110 fluminibus salices crassisque paludibus alni
nascuntur, steriles saxosis montibus orni;
litora myrtetis laetissima; denique apertos
Bacchus amat collis, Aquilonem et frigora taxi.
aspice et extremis domitum cultoribus orbem
Eoasque domos Arabum pictosque Gelonos:
divisae arboribus patriae. sola India nigrum
fert hebenum, solis est turea virga Sabaeis.
quid tibi odorato referam sudantia ligno
balsamaque et bacas semper frondentis acanthi?
120 quid nemora Aethiopum molli canentia lana,
velleraque ut foliis depectant tenuia Seres?
aut quos Oceano propior gerit India lucos,
extremi sinus orbis, ubi aëra vincere summum
arboris haud ullae iactu potuere sagittae?
et gens illa quidem sumptis non tarda pharetris.
Media fert tristis sucos tardumque saporem
felicis mali, quo non praesentius ullum,

purples and precocious vines, and how to sing
your glory, Rhaetic? (– but don't take on Falernia's
      cellars!)
There are Aminnean vines, wines fullest-bodied
to which the Tmolian and regal Phanean pay obeisance,
and the lesser Argitis, which none can rival
in prodigious juicing or long years persisting.   100
Nor would I overlook you, Rhodian vine, congenial to
      gods
and dessert courses, or Bumast with your buxom clusters.
But numberless variety, and numberless their names! –
nor profits it to apprehend their number:
who this would know would also seek to learn
how many sand-grains dervish in the Libyan desert's
      westwind
or, when the eastwind falls ferociously upon the ships,
to find how many Ionian swells break against the shore.

Nor truly can all soils support all growth.
Willows in rivers, in sludgy shoals alders   110
flourish, the fruitless ash on rocky slopes,
the shores are flush with myrtle, the vine loves
exposed hillsides, and the yew the chill northwind.
And mark the world, its distant verges tamed by yeomen:
the Arab's eastern homesteads, and the tattooed Scyths.
Trees have appointed homelands: only India begets
black ebony, only for the Sabaeans the frankincense sprig.
Why should I tell you of balsams dripping
from fragrant wood, or the seedpods of the ever-green
      acacia?
Why talk of Ethiopian groves white with woolly cotton,   120
or how from leaves China combs its silky integuments?
or, nearer the Abyss, what jungles India breeds,
wooded chambers at the world's extremes
where no arrow fired can surpass the air at treetop?
(Nor is that nation lazy handling their quivers!)
Media yields the sour juice and slow flavour
of the peptic citron, which – nothing more availing

pocula si quando saevae infecere novercae,
[   ]
130   auxilium venit ac membris agit atra venena.
ipsa ingens arbos faciemque simillima lauro,
et, si non alium late iactaret odorem,
laurus erat; folia haud ullis labentia ventis,
flos ad prima tenax; animas et olentia Medi
ora fovent illo et senibus medicantur anhelis.

Sed neque Medorum silvae, ditissima terra,
nec pulcher Ganges atque auro turbidus Hermus
laudibus Italiae certent, non Bactra neque Indi
totaque turiferis Panchaia pinguis harenis.
140   haec loca non tauri spirantes naribus ignem
invertere satis immanis dentibus hydri
nec galeis densisque virum seges horruit hastis;
sed gravidae fruges et Bacchi Massicus umor
implevere; tenent oleae armentaque laeta.
hinc bellator equus campo sese arduus infert,
hinc albi, Clitumne, greges et maxima taurus
victima, saepe tuo perfusi flumine sacro,
Romanos ad templa deum duxere triumphos.
hic ver adsiduum atque alienis mensibus aestas,
150   bis gravidae pecudes, bis pomis utilis arbos.
at rabidae tigres absunt et saeva leonum
semina, nec miseros fallunt aconita legentis,
nec rapit immensos orbis per humum neque tanto
squameus in spiram tractu se colligit anguis.
adde tot egregias urbes operumque laborem,
tot congesta manu praeruptis oppida saxis
fluminaque antiquos subterlabentia muros.
an mare, quod supra, memorem, quodque adluit infra?
anne lacus tantos? te, Lari maxime, teque,
160   fluctibus et fremitu adsurgens Benace marino?
an memorem portus Lucrinoque addita claustra
atque indignatum magnis stridoribus aequor,

when wicked stepmothers have poisoned thc draughts! –
comes as succour, and from the limbs drives the black
    dose.   130
Itself capacious, the tree in form recalls the bay
(and if it did not shed another scent, a bay it would be):
its leaves drop for no wind, its blossom singularly
clings, the Medes refresh their breaths with it
(their stinking mouths!) and treat their elders' asthma.

But neither Media, opulent in her woodlands,
nor the gorgeous Ganges, nor Hermus mazed with gold
can rival Italy's glories – neither Bactria nor India
nor Panchaia duned with thurifying sand.
Here no bulls with nostrils snorting flame   140
harrowed to plant a dragon's monstrous teeth,
no human harvest bristled up with helmets and serried
    spears,
but bursting fruits and Bacchus' Massic nectar
freight us, olives and fat flocks hold sway.
Here warhorses charge haughty on the field,
here white herds of bulls, the noblest sacrifice –
washed often by your holy waters, O Clitumnus –
have led Roman triumphs to the altars of the gods.
Here is spring eternal, and summer in unwonted months,
twice calve the cows, twice the tree is fit for fruit.   150
But nowhere raving tigers, nor the lion's savage brood,
no monkshood dupes hapless cullers,
nor darts the scaly snake his looping bulk across the marl
nor clenches his vast train up in a coil.
And reckon all the remarkable cities, monuments of toil,
so many towns heaped with hands upon stony steeps
with rivers underflowing ancient walls.
Should I mention the sea, laving the shore up north
and down south, or our great lakes? You, Como most
    splendid,
Benacus surging with swells and thunderous like the sea?   160
Should I mention ports, or the breakwater upon Lucrine,
or the water's roaring clamour at the affront

Iulia qua ponto longe sonat unda refuso
Tyrrhenusque fretis immittitur aestus Avernis?
haec eadem argenti rivos aerisque metalla
ostendit venis atque auro plurima fluxit.
haec genus acre virum, Marsos pubemque Sabellam
adsuetumque malo Ligurem Volscosque verutos
extulit, haec Decios, Marios, magnosque Camillos,
170   Scipiadas duros bello et te, maxime Caesar,
qui nunc extremis Asiae iam victor in oris
imbellem avertis Romanis arcibus Indum.
salve, magna parens frugum, Saturnia tellus,
magna virum: tibi res antiquae laudis et artem
ingredior, sanctos ausus recludere fontis,
Ascraeumque cano Romana per oppida carmen.

Nunc locus arvorum ingeniis, quae robora cuique,
quis color et quae sit rebus natura ferendis.
difficiles primum terrae collesque maligni,
180   tenuis ubi argilla et dumosis calculus arvis,
Palladia gaudent silva vivacis olivae.
indicio est tractu surgens oleaster eodem
plurimus et strati bacis silvestribus agri.
at quae pinguis humus dulcique uligine laeta,
quique frequens herbis et fertilis ubere campus
(qualem saepe cava montis convalle solemus
despicere; huc summis liquuntur rupibus amnes
felicemque trahunt limum) quique editus Austro
et filicem curvis invisam pascit aratris:
190   hic tibi praevalidas olim multoque fluentis
sufficiet Baccho vitis, hic fertilis uvae,
hic laticis, qualem pateris libamus et auro,
inflavit cum pinguis ebur Tyrrhenus ad aras,
lancibus et pandis fumantia reddimus exta.
sin armenta magis studium vitulosque tueri
aut ovium fetum aut urentis culta capellas,

where the Julian waves boom out as the bore gurges back
upon itself and the Tyrrhenian tide pours into Avernus
    froth?
This land flaunts her silver rills, the copper lode
in her veins, and with gold abundant flows.
She bore a flinty race of men – Marsians and the Sabine
    youth,
the Ligurian inured to plight, the Volscian dartmen,
Deciuses and Mariuses and mighty Camilluses,
war-tempered Scipios . . . and you, greatest Caesar,   170
who already victor on the farthest fronts of Asia now
fend the unwarlike Indian from the fortresses of Rome.
Hail exalted mother of fruits, Saturnian land,
exalted mother of men! For you the theme and craft
of ancient praise I undertake, daring to unseal the sacred
    springs
and sing through Roman plazas the song of Ascra.

Now for the character of soils, what strengths each has,
what colour and what properties for growth.
First, truculent earth and grudging hills
where's meagre clay and scree across the scrubby ground   180
thrill beneath Minerva's groves of long-enduring olive.
Its sign is oleaster thick upshooting through the tract,
the clunch strewn with wild berries.
But rich loam which luxuriates in sweet moisture,
a plot riot in greenery and fertile in nutrient
(as often we survey in sunken mountain swales
where from rimrocks melt runnels
dragging vital silt), which south-facing
fosters the fern, stymie of the curved plough:
this will soon supply you with hardiest vines   190
gushing in Dionysiac plenty, full of grapes
and of the wine we offer up from golden bowls
when the sleek Etruscan blows his ivory horn at altarside
and on bowed platters we oblate steaming entrails.
But if it's cattle and calves you choose to keep
or sheep to herd, or crop-spoiling goats,

saltus et saturi petito longinqua Tarenti,
et qualem infelix amisit Mantua campum
pascentem niveos herboso flumine cycnos:
200   non liquidi gregibus fontes, non gramina derunt,
et quantum longis carpent armenta diebus
exigua tantum gelidus ros nocte reponet.

Nigra fere et presso pinguis sub vomere terra
et cui putre solum (namque hoc imitamur arando)
optima frumentis: non ullo ex aequore cernes
plura domum tardis decedere plaustra iuvencis;
aut unde iratus silvam devexit arator
et nemora evertit multos ignava per annos,
antiquasque domos avium cum stirpibus imis
210   eruit; illae altum nidis petiere relictis,
at rudis enituit inpulso vomere campus.
nam ieiuna quidem clivosi glarea ruris
vix humilis apibus casias roremque ministrat,
et tofus scaber et nigris exesa chelydris
creta negant alios aeque serpentibus agros
dulcem ferre cibum et curvas praebere latebras.
quae tenuem exhalat nebulam fumosque volucris,
et bibit umorem et, cum volt, ex se ipsa remittit,
quaeque suo semper viridi se gramine vestit
220   nec scabie et salsa laedit robigine ferrum,
illa tibi laetis intexet vitibus ulmos,
illa ferax oleo est, illam experiere colendo
et facilem pecori et patientem vomeris unci.
talem dives arat Capua et vicina Vesaevo
ora iugo et vacuis Clanius non aequus Acerris.

*

make for the far-off glades of lush Tarentum
or pasture such as forlorn Mantua lost
which fed snow-white swans with its grassy brook:
neither clear water nor meadows will your flocks lack
    there,   200
and whatever the herds graze down during the long days
cold dews will replenish during the short nights.

Black humus, rich beneath the grubbing ploughshare
with crumbly soil (such soil we emulate with ploughing)
is usually best for grain. From no other field you'll see
more wagons retiring homeward behind cumbered bulls –
or where enraged the ploughman has ripped out the timber
and thrown down the groves, idle for long years,
the ancient homes of birds uptearing
at their deepest roots. They abandon nests and seek the
    sky,   210
but this rough thwaite will gleam beneath the
    ploughshare's burnish.
Then again, the starved gravel of hilly country
scarce sustains bees with lowly spurge and rosemary,
its chalk and crusty tufa gnawed away by black
    watersnakes
witness that no other lands provide to serpents
so sweet provender, nor proffer such sinuous lairs.
But soil that exhales thin mists and winding vapours,
that drinks up moisture, lets it out again with ease,
that ever decks itself in its own herbal green,
that galls not the iron with rot or salty rust –   220
such soil will wreathe in exuberant vines your elms,
will stream with olive oil, and as you'll find in tilling
will go easy on oxen and comply with the crooked share.
Bountiful Capua harrows such soil, and the coastal plain
beneath Vesuvius' ridge, and the banks of the Clanius,
unsparing of desolate Acerrae.

*

Nunc quo quamque modo possis cognoscere dicam.
rara sit an supra morem si densa requires
(altera frumentis quoniam favet, altera Baccho,
densa magis Cereri, rarissima quaeque Lyaeo),
230 ante locum capies oculis, alteque iubebis
in solido puteum demitti, omnemque repones
rursus humum et pedibus summas aequabis harenas.
si derunt, rarum pecorique et vitibus almis
aptius uber erit; sin in sua posse negabunt
ire loca et scrobibus superabit terra repletis,
spissus ager: glaebas cunctantis crassaque terga
exspecta et validis terram proscinde iuvencis.
salsa autem tellus et quae perhibetur amara
(frugibus infelix, ea nec mansuescit arando
240 nec Baccho genus aut pomis sua nomina servat),
tale dabit specimen: tu spisso vimine qualos
colaque prelorum fumosis deripe tectis;
huc ager ille malus dulcesque a fontibus undae
ad plenum calcentur; aqua eluctabitur omnis
scilicet, et grandes ibunt per vimina guttae;
at sapor indicium faciet manifestus, et ora
tristia temptantum sensu torquebit amaro.
pinguis item quae sit tellus, hoc denique pacto
discimus: haud umquam manibus iactata fatiscit,
250 sed picis in morem ad digitos lentescit habendo.
umida maiores herbas alit, ipsaque iusto
laetior. a! nimium ne sit mihi fertilis illa,
nec se praevalidam primis ostendat aristis!
quae gravis est ipso tacitam se pondere prodit,
quaeque levis. promptum est oculis praediscere nigram,
et quis cui color. at sceleratum exquirere frigus
difficile est: piceae tantum taxique nocentes
interdum aut hederae pandunt vestigia nigrae.

His animadversis terram multo ante memento
260 excoquere et magnos scrobibus concidere montis,
ante supinatas Aquiloni ostendere glaebas

Now I'll tell how you may recognize each soil.
If you wonder whether yours is lighter or more packed
    than most
(the one to corn is genial, the other to the vine –
compacted earth to Ceres, loosest soil to Bacchus),
first scout a site and bid a shaft be sunk to bedrock   230
then replace the dirt and stamp it flush along the brim.
If it comes up shy, your tilth is loose – more fit
for cattle and lavish vines. But if it refuses
to go down to level, if dirt's in surfeit when the pit refills,
your ground is thick: watch out for stubborn clods, stiff
ridges, and break up the earth with your strongest bulls.
But brackish ground, called bitter, bane to germination,
unmellowed by tillage, conserving not the lineage of vines,
the names of apples – it will give this proof: 240
fetch down from smoky rafters your tight-wickered
baskets and wine-strainers. Fill them with that worthless
    soil
tamped down, and spring-fresh sweetwater.
You'll see the water work through, great drops between
the willows, but its taste will testify, its bitter tang
will twist the taster's bittered tongue.
Rich earth we may discover this way only:
never does it crumble fretted in the hands
but pitchy sticks to fingers as it's handled.   250
Wet soil grows vegetation rank, itself unduly lush.
O! let my field not be that too-fertile earth,
nor show too potent with the nascent ears.
Heavy soil betrays itself in silence by its weight,
and so does light. It's easy to figure black soil
at a glance, or any colour, but to detect the profane chill
is hard: only pitch-pines, toxic yew trees,
or sometimes black ivies give inkling of its stain.

These things noted, remember long ahead to sunbake
your land, to gouge trenches through the larger swells,   260
to expose the clods upturned to the northwind

quam laetum infodias vitis genus. optima putri
arva solo: id venti curant gelidaeque pruinae
et labefacta movens robustus iugera fossor.
at si quos haud ulla viros vigilantia fugit,
ante locum similem exquirunt, ubi prima paretur
arboribus seges et quo mox digesta feratur,
mutatam ignorent subito ne semina matrem.
quin etiam caeli regionem in cortice signant,
270 ut quo quaeque modo steterit, qua parte calores
austrinos tulerit, quae terga obverterit axi,
restituant: adeo in teneris consuescere multum est.

Collibus an plano melius sit ponere vitem,
quaere prius. si pinguis agros metabere campi,
densa sere: in denso non segnior ubere Bacchus;
sin tumulis acclive solum collisque supinos,
indulge ordinibus; nec setius omnis in unguem
arboribus positis secto via limite quadret.
ut saepe ingenti bello cum longa cohortis
280 explicuit legio et campo stetit agmen aperto,
derectaeque acies, ac late fluctuat omnis
aere renidenti tellus, necdum horrida miscent
proelia, sed dubius mediis Mars errat in armis:
omnia sint paribus numeris dimensa viarum,
non animum modo uti pascat prospectus inanem,
sed quia non aliter viris dabit omnibus aequas
terra, neque in vacuum poterunt se extendere rami.

Forsitan et scrobibus quae sint fastigia quaeras.
ausim vel tenui vitem committere sulco;

before you plant the vine's blithe stock. The best
    ploughland
has crumbling soil: this the winds worry over, and the wintry
frosts, and the burly digger who rousts and roughs your
    acres.
But men whose vigilance nothing slips
first seek out twinned fields, one where early the crop be
    nursed
up to trees, and one where later transplants be arrayed
lest seedlings balk unrecognizing at their mother-soil's
sudden change. In fact, that they might reproduce each
    stalk's
celestial bearings, they mark on its bark which side
    endured   270
southern heats, and where its back toward the North Pole
    turned,
so powerfully runs habit in the tender stems.

Whether best to set the vine on hills or plain
study first to know. If rich prairie earth you survey,
plant closely: in close companies never sluggish fruits the
    vine.
But if a down of mounds upsloped and couchant hills,
loosen your rows – but still let every path, when trees
are set, square plumb with each cross-path intersecting.
As often in great battle, when long the legion has deployed
its cohort down the open field, the column halted,   280
frontline taut, and far the landscape ripples
with gleaming bronze, the horrid scrimmage
not yet joined, but undecided Mars ranges among the
    ranks:
just so let all your paths be measured out in equal span,
not merely that the view may ravish idle fancy
but because not else will the earth give equal vigour
to all, nor can the branches flare themselves in empty air.

Perhaps you wonder what depth should be your digging.
I'd dare commit the vine even to a shallow furrow,

290   altior ac penitus terrae defigitur arbos,
      aesculus in primis, quae quantum vertice ad auras
      aetherias, tantum radice in Tartara tendit.
      ergo non hiemes illam, non flabra neque imbres
      convellunt; immota manet, multosque nepotes,
      multa virum volvens durando saecula vincit.
      tum fortis late ramos et bracchia tendens
      huc illuc, media ipsa ingentem sustinet umbram.

      Neve tibi ad solem vergant vineta cadentem,
      neve inter vitis corylum sere, neve flagella
300   summa pete aut summa defringe ex arbore plantas
      (tantus amor terrae), neu ferro laede retunso
      semina, neve oleae silvestris insere truncos.
      nam saepe incautis pastoribus excidit ignis,
      qui furtim pingui primum sub cortice tectus
      robora conprendit, frondesque elapsus in altas
      ingentem caelo sonitum dedit; inde secutus
      per ramos victor perque alta cacumina regnat
      et totum involvit flammis nemus et ruit atram
      ad caelum picea crassus caligine nubem,
310   praesertim si tempestas a vertice silvis
      incubuit, glomeratque ferens incendia ventus.
      hoc ubi, non a stirpe valent caesaeque reverti
      possunt atque ima similes revirescere terra;
      infelix superat foliis oleaster amaris.

      Nec tibi tam prudens quisquam persuadeat auctor
      tellurem Borea rigidam spirante movere.
      rura gelu tunc claudit hiems nec semine iacto
      concretam patitur radicem adfigere terrae.
      optima vinetis satio, cum vere rubente
320   candida venit avis longis invisa colubris,
      prima vel autumni sub frigora, cum rapidus Sol
      nondum hiemem contingit equis, iam praeterit aestas.
      ver adeo frondi nemorum, ver utile silvis;

but deeper down inside the earth is rooted its support-tree, 290
the oak above all, which as far thrusts its top toward
the breath of heaven as pokes its roots to Hell.
Thus no squall, no drench nor gales uptear it.
Unshaken it stands, enduring it outlasts unnumbered
generations and ages of men, scrolling them by
while its stout branches stretching wide, its arms
splayed everywhere, axial it hoists a massive shade.

Neither let your vineyard slope toward the setting sun
nor plant hazel among the vines, nor poll the highest
switches nor swipe cuttings from the treetop   300
(they love the earth too much!), nor with the dulled
        pruning hook
wound plantlings. Don't graft into wild olive-trunks,
for often from careless shepherds falls a spark
which furtive lurking first beneath the oily bark
seizes the heartwood, and slipping to the leaves overhead
skyward sends a thunderous roar, then chasing
through the branches vanquishes the treetops, a conqueror,
and shrouds the grove entire in flame, and vomits
upward puffs smutty with pitch-thick murk,
most if dirty weather from the ether stoops   310
sheer to the forest, its churning winds winding up a fireball.
In this event, the stock serves not the vines, which clipped
cannot revive nor sunk in earth resume their former green:
only the baneful oleaster with its bitter leaves survives.

Let no sage seem so cunning to persuade you
to work the hard dirt while the northwind moans.
Then with frost winter grips the land, and suffers not
the set seedling to secure its frozen root in soil.
Best time for planting vines is when in spring's blush
the white stork appears, foe to trailing snakes,   320
or nigh on autumn's first frost, when the blazing sun
already blown past summer has not yet nuzzled winter
        with his team.
O spring the leafy groves, spring the forest speeds,

vere tument terrae et genitalia semina poscunt.
tum pater omnipotens fecundis imbribus Aether
coniugis in gremium laetae descendit et omnis
magnus alit magno commixtus corpore fetus.
avia tum resonant avibus virgulta canoris
et Venerem certis repetunt armenta diebus;
330   parturit almus ager Zephyrique tepentibus auris
laxant arva sinus; superat tener omnibus umor,
inque novos soles audent se gramina tuto
credere, nec metuit surgentis pampinus Austros
aut actum caelo magnis Aquilonibus imbrem,
sed trudit gemmas et frondes explicat omnis.
non alios prima crescentis origine mundi
inluxisse dies aliumve habuisse tenorem
crediderim: ver illud erat, ver magnus agebat
orbis et hibernis parcebant flatibus Euri,
340   cum primae lucem pecudes hausere, virumque
terrea progenies duris caput extulit arvis,
immissaeque ferae silvis et sidera caelo.
nec res hunc tenerae possent perferre laborem,
si non tanta quies iret frigusque caloremque
inter, et exciperet caeli indulgentia terras.

Quod superest, quaecumque premes virgulta per agros,
sparge fimo pingui et multa memor occule terra.
aut lapidem bibulum aut squalentis infode conchas;
inter enim labentur aquae, tenuisque subibit
350   halitus atque animos tollent sata. iamque reperti,
qui saxo super atque ingentis pondere testae
urgerent: hoc effusos munimen ad imbris,
hoc, ubi hiulca siti findit canis aestifer arva.

Seminibus positis superest diducere terram
saepius ad capita et duros iactare bidentis,

in spring the acres swell and beg for pregnant seed.
Then Heaven, almighty Father, in vital showers comes
    down
into the lap of his ecstatic bride, where his potence
with her potent loins commingling engenders all
    florescence.
Then trackless thickets trill with birdsong
and in their hour appointed the herds renew the rut.
Bountiful broods the earth and under warm westerlies   330
the fields unloose their bosom – soft moisture soaks into
    everything
and the cotyledons dare resign themselves to the new suns,
the shoots fear not the southwind's surge
nor showers driven through the sky by the gusting North,
but push out buds and all their leaves unfold.
Such days, I fancy, dawned upon the birth
of the infant earth, and such a course they kept:
spring it was, spring the wide world observed –
the eastwinds spared their wintry blasts,
when first the cattle drank in light, and the earthen line   340
of men reared up its head from the stiff fields
and beasts were released to forests and stars released to
    sky.
Frail things could not endure this world's trials
did not so long a respite come between the heats
and frosts, did not heaven's clemency reprieve the earth.

What's more, what slips you set in your fields
smear with rich dung, and mind you bury them deep in soil.
Plant them with leaching stones or jagged shells,
for water will seep out between, and slight the air
slip in, and the crop will perk up. Some have been known   350
to lean a rock upon them, or a heavy jar, a shield
against downpours or when the fevered Dog Star cracks
    the earth.

The seedlings set, it's left to break up soil, often,
to the roots, to swing the sturdy mattock or to work

aut presso exercere solum sub vomere et ipsa
flectere luctantis inter vineta iuvencos;
tum levis calamos et rasae hastilia virgae
fraxineasque aptare sudes furcasque valentis,
360   viribus eniti quarum et contemnere ventos
adsuescant summasque sequi tabulata per ulmos.

Ac dum prima novis adolescit frondibus aetas,
parcendum teneris, et dum se laetus ad auras
palmes agit laxis per purum immissus habenis,
ipsa acie nondum falcis temptanda, sed uncis
carpendae manibus frondes interque legendae.
inde ubi iam validis amplexae stirpibus ulmos
exierint, tum stringe comas, tum bracchia tonde
(ante reformidant ferrum), tum denique dura
370   exerce imperia et ramos compesce fluentis.

Texendae saepes etiam et pecus omne tenendum,
praecipue dum frons tenera imprudensque laborum;
cui super indignas hiemes solemque potentem
silvestres uri adsidue capreaeque sequaces
inludunt, pascuntur oves avidaeque iuvencae.
frigora nec tantum cana concreta pruina
aut gravis incumbens scopulis arentibus aestas,
quantum illi nocuere greges durique venenum
dentis et admorso signata in stirpe cicatrix.
380   non aliam ob culpam Baccho caper omnibus aris
caeditur et veteres ineunt proscaenia ludi,
praemiaque ingeniis pagos et compita circum
Thesidae posuere, atque inter pocula laeti
mollibus in pratis unctos saluere per utres.
nec non Ausonii, Troia gens missa, coloni
versibus incomptis ludunt risuque soluto,
oraque corticibus sumunt horrenda cavatis,
et te, Bacche, vocant per carmina laeta, tibique

the earth beneath the ploughshare's push, and steer
your struggling steers between the vinerows. Then prepare
smooth reeds and shafts of peeled wood, ash stakes
strong and forked, with whose support
the vines will learn to climb, to scoff at winds,   360
to course to the elm-tops limb by limb.

While their first growth fledges in new leaves
spare their tenderness, and while gleefully heavenward
the shoot spurts, rushing unbridled through the air,
don't yet attack with the pruning edge, but with pinching
fingers pick the leaves and thin them out.
Later, when they've thrived, circling the elms
with lusty bine, *then* clip their tresses, *then* dock their arms
(earlier, and they'll shrink from the knife), then last install
an iron command and curb the streaming branches.   370

Weave hedges, too, and altogether bar the flocks,
most of all while leaves are tender, unacquainted with
        strain.
For besides winter's indignities and the tyrant sun,
wild oxen ever romp in them, and pestering goats,
and sheep and heifers voracious graze them down.
Not winter stiff with hoar frost, not summer
leaning heavy upon scorched rocks
so ravage them as herds do, with their rough and pestilent
teeth, the scar graved into the gnawed stem.
For no fault else a goat is slaughtered at every altar   380
to Bacchus. For this, time-honoured tragedies take the
        stage.
For this, Theseus' Athenian sons established prizes for wit
in the village-commons and at crossroads, and in their cups
        gaily
capered upon oiled goatskins in the meadows soft.
Just so Ausonian farmers, colonists sent out from Troy,
roister with uncouth verse, and with laughter unrestrained,
and don horrific masks of concave bark
and invoke you, O Bacchus, in songs exultant, and to you

oscilla ex alta suspendunt mollia pinu.
390 hinc omnis largo pubescit vinea fetu,
complentur vallesque cavae saltusque profundi
et quocumque deus circum caput egit honestum.
ergo rite suum Baccho dicemus honorem
carminibus patriis lancesque et liba feremus,
et ductus cornu stabit sacer hircus ad aram,
pinguiaque in veribus torrebimus exta colurnis.

Est etiam ille labor curandis vitibus alter,
cui numquam exhausti satis est: namque omne quotannis
terque quaterque solum scindendum glaebaque versis
400 aeternum frangenda bidentibus, omne levandum
fronde nemus. redit agricolis labor actus in orbem,
atque in se sua per vestigia volvitur annus.
ac iam olim, seras posuit cum vinea frondes,
frigidus et silvis Aquilo decussit honorem,
iam tum acer curas venientem extendit in annum
rusticus, et curvo Saturni dente relictam
persequitur vitem attondens fingitque putando.
primus humum fodito, primus devecta cremato
sarmenta et vallos primus sub tecta referto;
410 postremus metito. bis vitibus ingruit umbra,
bis segetem densis obducunt sentibus herbae;
durus uterque labor: laudato ingentia rura,
exiguum colito. nec non etiam aspera rusci
vimina per silvam et ripis fluvialis harundo
caeditur, incultique exercet cura salicti.
iam vinctae vites, iam falcem arbusta reponunt,
iam canit effectos extremus vinitor antes:
sollicitanda tamen tellus pulvisque movendus,
et iam maturis metuendus Iuppiter uvis.

*

hang waxen effigies from the towering pine.
Hence every vineyard ripens with a largesse of fruit,   390
the glens and hollows fill to bursting
everywhere the god swivels his august countenance.
To Bacchus, then, we'll chant his anthems due,
our homeland hymns, and cakes and platters bring,
as led by the horn the consecrated goat stands altarside
whose rich organs we will roast upon spits of hazel.

There's too that other chore maintaining vines,
on which never enough effort is spent: for thrice or four
    times yearly
must all soil be gouged open, and the clods with a clawed
    mattock
ceaselessly broken up, and the grove unburdened   400
of all foliage. Toil wheels back to the farmer, cycling
as the year rolls back over its own tracks.
Even when the vineyard has laid down its late leaves
and cold the northwind's shaken from the woods their glory,
even then the keen farmhand stretches forth his
    stewardship
to the coming year, and with Saturn's hooked sickle pursues
the unmeddled vine, cropping and pruning to shape it.
Be first to dig the earth, first to burn the hauled-out
brushwood, first to store sheltered your vine-stakes –
but last to reap. Twice upon the vines floods the shade,   410
twice weeds thick with brambles choke the crop,
brutal each chore! *Praise a vast estate,*
till a small one. And more, gnarled broom-shoots
from the woods and from the riverbanks the reeds
are cut, and care of the wild willow-stand taxes us.
At last the vines are bound, at last the vineyard discharges
the pruning-hook, and the last vinedresser sings his finished
    rows:
still the ground must be harassed, the soil stirred
and the skies misdoubted by the now-ripe grapes.

*

420 Contra non ulla est oleis cultura, neque illae
procurvam exspectant falcem rastrosque tenacis,
cum semel haeserunt arvis aurasque tulerunt;
ipsa satis tellus, cum dente recluditur unco,
sufficit umorem et gravidas, cum vomere, fruges.
hoc pinguem et placitam Paci nutritor olivam.

Poma quoque, ut primum truncos sensere valentis
et viris habuere suas, ad sidera raptim
vi propria nituntur opisque haud indiga nostrae.
nec minus interea fetu nemus omne gravescit,
430 sanguineisque inculta rubent aviaria bacis.
tondentur cytisi, taedas silva alta ministrat,
pascunturque ignes nocturni et lumina fundunt.
[   ]
quid maiora sequar? salices humilesque genestae
aut illae pecori frondem aut pastoribus umbram
sufficiunt saepemque satis et pabula melli.
et iuvat undantem buxo spectare Cytorum
Naryciaeque picis lucos, iuvat arva videre
non rastris, hominum non ulli obnoxia curae.
440 ipsae Caucasio steriles in vertice silvae,
quas animosi Euri adsidue franguntque feruntque,
dant alios aliae fetus, dant utile lignum
navigiis pinus, domibus cedrumque cupressosque;
hinc radios trivere rotis, hinc tympana plaustris
agricolae, et pandas ratibus posuere carinas.
viminibus salices fecundae, frondibus ulmi,
at myrtus validis hastilibus et bona bello
cornus, Ituraeos taxi torquentur in arcus.
nec tiliae leves aut torno rasile buxum
450 non formam accipiunt ferroque cavantur acuto.
nec non et torrentem undam levis innatat alnus

By contrast, olives need no tending, nor look they   420
for the billhook or the grasping hoe
when once they've rooted in the fields and braved the
     winds.
Earth on her own, when opened by the hoe's tooth or the
     plough,
yields ample moisture and breeds abundant fruits.
So nurture the olive, plump favourite of Peace.

Fruit trees too, when first they feel their trunks are sturdy
and assume their strength, nimbly to the stars
with native force surge, needing no push from us.
No less each woodland swells with fruit,
and with blood-red berries blush the wild bird haunts.   430
There's clover for grazing. The high forest supplies pine,
the fires of night are fed and flood with light.
Why grander themes pursue? – Willows and the homely
     broom
offer browse for flocks or shepherd's shade,
a hedge around crops and nectar for honey.
What joy to behold Cytorus waving with box-trees
and Naryx with groves of pine, what joy to gaze on fields
beholden to no rake, nor to any man for care!
Even fruitless trees along the summits of the Caucasus,   440
which blustering eastwinds ever rip and ransack,
yield each a different product, yield handy timber:
pines for ships, cedar and cypress for houses.
From these spoked wheels, from these drum-wheels for
     wagons
farmers fashion, from these they frame bowed keels for
     ships.
Willows are prolific in wicker, elms in leaves,
but the myrtle and scrappy cornel both bloom sturdy
     spearshafts,
and yews are wrested into Ituraean bows.
Smooth linden and box-wood shaved on the lathe
assume their shape, tooled out with sharp iron.   450
Over the torrent's froth paddles the light alder

missa Pado, nec non et apes examina condunt
corticibusque cavis vitiosaeque ilicis alvo.
quid memorandum aeque Baccheia dona tulerunt?
Bacchus et ad culpam causas dedit; ille furentis
Centauros leto domuit, Rhoetumque Pholumque
et magno Hylaeum Lapithis cratere minantem.

O fortunatos nimium, sua si bona norint,
agricolas! quibus ipsa procul discordibus armis
460   fundit humo facilem victum iustissima tellus.
si non ingentem foribus domus alta superbis
mane salutantum totis vomit aedibus undam,
nec varios inhiant pulchra testudine postis
inlusasque auro vestes Ephyreiaque aera,
alba neque Assyrio fucatur lana veneno,
nec casia liquidi corrumpitur usus olivi?
at secura quies et nescia fallere vita,
dives opum variarum, at latis otia fundis,
speluncae vivique lacus et frigida Tempe
470   mugitusque boum mollesque sub arbore somni
non absunt; illic saltus ac lustra ferarum,
et patiens operum exiguoque adsueta iuventus,
sacra deum sanctique patres: extrema per illos
Iustitia excedens terris vestigia fecit.

Me vero primum dulces ante omnia Musae,
quarum sacra fero ingenti percussus amore,
accipiant caelique vias et sidera monstrent,
defectus solis varios lunaeque labores;

launched upon the Po, and bees aswarm hive
in burrowed bark or the rotten heart of a holm oak.
What so wondrous have the gifts of Bacchus borne?
In truth, Bacchus has given us grounds to reproach him, for
  he
overmastered the wine-raged Centaurs unto death, Rhoetus
  and Pholus
and Hylaeus too, who menaced the Lapiths with a giant
  flagon.

O blessed farmers! doubly blessed if they should recognize
their blessings! For whom far from clashing arms
the just earth pours from her soil easy provision.   460
What if no mansion, lofty with lordly doors, disgorges
each dawn from all quarters a grand tide of callers?
What if they never gawk at doorposts freaked with
  tortoiseshell
resplendent, or raiment tricked with gold, or Corinthian
  bronzes?
What if their white wool's never stained with Assyrian
  potions,
their pure oil not defiled with cinnamon?
Still there's a carefree peace, and life unversed in guile,
a wealth of varied plenty, still the leisure of broad estates –
caves and natural lakes and Tempes cool,
lowing cows and soft sleep beneath the trees   470
are never wanting. There are pastured glens and game-runs,
there youth accustomed to industry and seasoned by
  dearth,
there devotion to gods and filial piety: among these
departing Justice left her last footprints upon the earth.

But as for me, O first may the Muses – sovereign sweet!
whose mysteries I observe struck through with boundless
  love! –
receive me, show me the starry paths of heaven,
the sun's eclipses and the moon's marbled travails,

unde tremor terris, qua vi maria alta tumescant
480 obicibus ruptis rursusque in se ipsa residant,
quid tantum Oceano properent se tinguere soles
hiberni, vel quae tardis mora noctibus obstet.
sin, has ne possim naturae accedere partis,
frigidus obstiterit circum praecordia sanguis,
rura mihi et rigui placeant in vallibus amnes,
flumina amem silvasque inglorius. o ubi campi
Spercheosque et virginibus bacchata Lacaenis
Taygeta! o qui me gelidis convallibus Haemi
sistat et ingenti ramorum protegat umbra!

490 Felix, qui potuit rerum cognoscere causas,
atque metus omnis et inexorabile fatum
subiecit pedibus strepitumque Acherontis avari.
fortunatus et ille, deos qui novit agrestis,
Panaque Silvanumque senem Nymphasque sorores.
illum non populi fasces, non purpura regum
flexit et infidos agitans discordia fratres,
aut coniurato descendens Dacus ab Histro,
non res Romanae perituraque regna; neque ille
aut doluit miserans inopem aut invidit habenti.
500 quos rami fructus, quos ipsa volentia rura
sponte tulere sua, carpsit, nec ferrea iura
insanumque forum aut populi tabularia vidit.
sollicitant alii remis freta caeca, ruuntque
in ferrum, penetrant aulas et limina regum;
hic petit excidiis urbem miserosque penatis,
ut gemma bibat et Sarrano dormiat ostro;
condit opes alius defossoque incubat auro;
hic stupet attonitus rostris; hunc plausus hiantem
per cuneos geminatus enim plebisque patrumque

at which the earth quakes, under whose force the seas swell
   high
bursting their bounds, and swirl back upon themselves,   480
why winter suns so haste to plunge themselves
in Ocean, what delay stays the dragging winter nights . . .
But if I cannot plumb these realms of nature,
if the chill blood circling my heart thwarts me,
let the land be my delight, the streams that irrigate the
   vales,
the rills and forests let me love unsung. O where the plains,
the Spercheus, Mount Taygetus turned bacchanal by
   Spartan girls?!
O who will set me in the cool dells of Haemus
and canopy me with the branches' sprawling shade?!

O happy he who can fathom the causes of things,   490
who's thrown all fear and dogged Fate
beneath his feet, and the roaring of ravenous Acheron.
And blessed is he conversant with the rustic gods,
Pan and stooped Silvanus and the Nymphs' sisterhood.
Him no public commendation, no kingly purple
swerves, nor strife churning brothers to treachery,
nor Dacians swooping in cahoots with Danube
nor Roman affairs and wasting regimes,
nor grieves he pitying the poor or grudging the rich.
The fruit his branches, his own lands freely offer up   500
and eagerly, he plucks. But never has he seen
the iron laws, the lunatic Forum, the office of public
   records.
Others fret with oars uncharted seas, or rush
upon the sword, or infiltrate the courts and vestibules of
   kings.
One visits devastation on a city and its wretched hearths
that he may slurp from a jewelled cup and snore on Tyrian
   purple.
Another hoards treasure and broods over buried gold.
One wonders thunderstruck at the podium, one gapes
transported by the applause of senators and commonfolk

510   corripuit; gaudent perfusi sanguine fratrum,
       exsilioque domos et dulcia limina mutant
       atque alio patriam quaerunt sub sole iacentem.

       Agricola incurvo terram dimovit aratro:
       hinc anni labor, hinc patriam parvosque nepotes
       sustinet, hinc armenta boum meritosque iuvencos.
       nec requies, quin aut pomis exuberet annus
       aut fetu pecorum aut Cerealis mergite culmi,
       proventuque oneret sulcos atque horrea vincat.
       venit hiems: teritur Sicyonia baca trapetis,
520   glande sues laeti redeunt, dant arbuta silvae;
       et varios ponit fetus autumnus, et alte
       mitis in apricis coquitur vindemia saxis.
       interea dulces pendent circum oscula nati,
       casta pudicitiam servat domus, ubera vaccae
       lactea demittunt, pinguesque in gramine laeto
       inter se adversis luctantur cornibus haedi.
       ipse dies agitat festos fususque per herbam,
       ignis ubi in medio et socii cratera coronant,
       te libans, Lenaee, vocat pecorisque magistris
530   velocis iaculi certamina ponit in ulmo,
       corporaque agresti nudant praedura palaestrae.

       Hanc olim veteres vitam coluere Sabini,
       hanc Remus et frater, sic fortis Etruria crevit
       scilicet et rerum facta est pulcherrima Roma,
       septemque una sibi muro circumdedit arces.
       ante etiam sceptrum Dictaei regis et ante
       impia quam caesis gens est epulata iuvencis,

resounding through the galleries. Drenched in their
    brothers' blood,   510
they exult, and trade exile for their homes and sweet
    porches,
and seek a homeland under an alien sun.

The farmer has split the earth with the curving plough:
hence springs his year's work, hence his nation and small
    grandsons
he sustains, his cattle herds and trusty bullocks.
No respite: why, the season teems with fruits,
or the herd's calves, or with sheaves of cornstalks,
their harvest freighting furrows and bursting granaries.
Come winter, Sicyon's olive is crushed in the press,
the hogs return fatted with acorns, and the forests tender
    arbutes.   520
Autumn, too, lays out its sundry produce, and up
on sunlit rocks basks the mellowing vintage.
Meanwhile his dear children hang upon his kisses,
his virtuous home protects its purity, the cows
droop milky udders, and fat upon the fertile paddock
with horns opposed kids tussle among themselves.
The farmer himself keeps holidays, and sprawled upon the
    grass,
when his friends ring the bonfire and wreathe the bowl,
pouring his libation he invokes you, winepress god, and for
    his shepherds
nails upon the elm a contest for the fleet javelin   530
while rustics strip their muscled brawn for wrestling.

Such a life once lived the ancient Sabines,
such Remus and his brother. So too Etruria waxed in
    strength
and Rome is become the fairest of things,
circling seven hills with its single wall.
Even before the sceptred sway of Jupiter, Dictaean king,
    before
a godless race feasted on slaughtered steers,

aureus hanc vitam in terris Saturnus agebat;
necdum etiam audierant inflari classica, necdum
540   impositos duris crepitare incudibus ensis.

Sed nos inmensum spatiis confecimus aequor,
et iam tempus equum fumantia solvere colla.

such a life golden Saturn led on earth:
none yet had heard the bugle blare, nor yet
swords clank, struck on iron anvils.   540

But we on our way have run a vast expanse.
Now's time to unharness the horses' steaming necks.

Book Three

LIBER III

Te quoque, magna Pales, et te memorande canemus
pastor ab Amphryso, vos, silvae amnesque Lycaei.
cetera, quae vacuas tenuissent carmine mentes,
omnia iam volgata: quis aut Eurysthea durum
aut inlaudati nescit Busiridis aras?
cui non dictus Hylas puer et Latonia Delos
Hippodameque umeroque Pelops insignis eburno,
acer equis? temptanda via est, qua me quoque possim
tollere humo victorque virum volitare per ora.
10 primus ego in patriam mecum, modo vita supersit,
Aonio rediens deducam vertice Musas;
primus Idumaeas referam tibi, Mantua, palmas,
et viridi in campo templum de marmore ponam
propter aquam, tardis ingens ubi flexibus errat
Mincius et tenera praetexit harundine ripas.
in medio mihi Caesar erit templumque tenebit.
illi victor ego et Tyrio conspectus in ostro
centum quadriiugos agitabo ad flumina currus.
cuncta mihi, Alpheum linquens lucosque Molorchi,
20 cursibus et crudo decernet Graecia caestu.
ipse caput tonsae foliis ornatus olivae
dona feram. iam nunc sollemnis ducere pompas

BOOK THREE

You too great Pales we sing, and you renowned
O goatherd god of Amphrysus, and you Lycaean woods
    and rills.
Other themes which might have idle fancies charmed with
    song
all hackneyed now: who hasn't heard
of ruthless Eurystheus, or the altars of reviled Busiris?
Who hasn't rehashed the boy Hylas and Latona's Delos,
Hippodamia and Pelops conspicuous with his ivory
    shoulder,
shrewd with his team? I must essay a path by which I too
may rise from earth a triumph fluttering on the lips of men.
I first, if only life prolong, into my country returning   10
will lead the Muses from the Aonian mount,
I first will bear the palms of Idumaea, Mantua, back to you
and in the green field a marble temple plant
at water's edge, where in slow turns wanders
great Mincius fringing its banks with supple reeds.
In its nave I will have Caesar, and he will have its
    dominion.
In his honour I, a victor dazzling in Tyrian purple,
will drive a hundred quadrigs along the river.
For me, forsaking Alpheus and the Nemean groves
all Greece upon the racetrack will compete, and in rawhide
    gloves.   20
My temples trimmed with clipped olive leaves,
I'll bring the offering. Even now I'd joy to lead the ritual

     ad delubra iuvat caesosque videre iuvencos,
     vel scaena ut versis discedat frontibus utque
     purpurea intexti tollant aulaea Britanni.
     in foribus pugnam ex auro solidoque elephanto
     Gangaridum faciam victorisque arma Quirini,
     atque hic undantem bello magnumque fluentem
     Nilum ac navali surgentis aere columnas.
30   addam urbes Asiae domitas pulsumque Niphaten
     fidentemque fuga Parthum versisque sagittis,
     et duo rapta manu diverso ex hoste tropaea
     bisque triumphatas utroque ab litore gentes.
     stabunt et Parii lapides, spirantia signa,
     Assaraci proles demissaeque ab Iove gentis
     nomina, Trosque parens et Troiae Cynthius auctor.
     Invidia infelix Furias amnemque severum
     Cocyti metuet tortosque Ixionis anguis
     immanemque rotam et non exsuperabile saxum.

40   Interea Dryadum silvas saltusque sequamur
     intactos, tua, Maecenas, haud mollia iussa.
     te sine nil altum mens incohat. en age, segnis
     rumpe moras; vocat ingenti clamore Cithaeron
     Taygetique canes domitrixque Epidaurus equorum,
     et vox adsensu nemorum ingeminata remugit.
     mox tamen ardentis accingar dicere pugnas
     Caesaris et nomen fama tot ferre per annos,
     Tithoni prima quot abest ab origine Caesar.

*

procession to the sanctuary, to watch the bullocks'
    sacrifice,
or see the stage-scene vanish when the sets are turned,
how its embroidered Britons lift the purple curtain.
Upon the doors in gold and solid ivory will I work
the battle of the Ganges hordes, the arms of our
    conquering Romulus,
and here billowing with war and flowing full
the Nile, and fleets rigged high with bronze.
I will add Asian cities overthrown, and routed Niphates,   30
the Parthian so cocky in his dodging and back-flung
    arrows,
our two trophies snatched by force from foes to East and
    West,
twice vanquished the nations on two shores.
And here will stand Parian statuary, breathing images:
the line of Assaracus, the great names of this Jove-sprung
race, patriarch Tros and the Cynthian architect of Troy.
Contemptible Envy will quake before the Furies and the
    severe
stream of Cocytus, before Ixion's knotted snakes
and monstrous wheel, before the insurmountable stone.

Meanwhile the dryads' virgin woods and glades let us
    pursue,   40
Maecenas, though no sinecure your charge.
Without you my mind attempts nothing sublime: up then,
cut short this laggard stay! With rowdy clamour Cithaeron
    calls
and the hounds of Taygetus, and horse-taming Epidaurus –
the cry reverberates, redoubled in the groves' huzzahs.
But soon I'll gird myself to sing the blazing campaigns
of Caesar, to trumpet his name in glory through as many
    years
as ticked away from the ancient birth of Tithonus to
    Caesar.

*

Seu quis Olympiacae miratus praemia palmae
50   pascit equos, seu quis fortis ad aratra iuvencos,
corpora praecipue matrum legat. optima torvae
forma bovis, cui turpe caput, cui plurima cervix,
et crurum tenus a mento palearia pendent;
tum longo nullus lateri modus; omnia magna,
pes etiam; et camuris hirtae sub cornibus aures.
nec mihi displiceat maculis insignis et albo,
aut iuga detractans interdumque aspera cornu
et faciem tauro propior, quaeque ardua tota
et gradiens ima verrit vestigia cauda.
60   aetas Lucinam iustosque pati hymenaeos
desinit ante decem, post quattuor incipit annos;
cetera nec feturae habilis nec fortis aratris.
interea, superat gregibus dum laeta iuventas,
solve mares; mitte in Venerem pecuaria primus,
atque aliam ex alia generando suffice prolem.
optima quaeque dies miseris mortalibus aevi
prima fugit; subeunt morbi tristisque senectus
et labor, et durae rapit inclementia mortis.
semper erunt, quarum mutari corpora malis:
70   semper enim refice ac, ne post amissa requiras,
anteveni et subolem armento sortire quotannis.

Nec non et pecori est idem delectus equino.
tu modo, quos in spem statues submittere gentis,
praecipuum iam inde a teneris impende laborem.
continuo pecoris generosi pullus in arvis
altius ingreditur et mollia crura reponit;
primus et ire viam et fluvios temptare minaces
audet et ignoto sese committere ponti,
nec vanos horret strepitus. illi ardua cervix
80   argutumque caput, brevis alvus obesaque terga,
luxuriatque toris animosum pectus. honesti

Whether admiring the prize of Olympic palms
one breeds horses, or rather strong steers for the plough,   50
let him study foremost the cast of the dam. The best cow
is fierce of feature, whose head is ugly, neck thick,
dewlaps hanging from chin to shins,
no end to her broad flank, big all over,
even her feet, with shaggy ears under crooked horns.
Nor would I reject her brindled with glaring white,
or shirking the yoke, or odd times ornery with the horn,
face more like a bull, tall throughout,
who ambling drags her tail-tip in her track.
The age for childbirth and formal wedlock   60
passes by the tenth year, begins beyond the fourth,
the rest of her years not fit to calve nor strong for the
      plough.
Meantime, while in the herds frisky youth prevails
turn loose the males – be first to send your cattle to rut
and by breeding bring forth stock after stock.
All life's best days speed earliest away
to mortal rue; in slink diseases, bleak dotage
and distress, and cruel death ravages unmerciful.
Always there'll be cows whose looks you'd rather trade
      away:
always replace them, and – lest later you lament your
      losses –   70
plan ahead, choosing yearly new calves to build your herd.

No different the selection for your stud of horses.
Only to those whom you resolve to rear as the hope
of the herd devote special pains, right from their
      tenderness.
From the first the pure-bred foal in the paddock
prances high and dainty sets his hooves,
first to stride the path, to brave perilous rivers,
he dares to commit himself to an unknown bridge
and spooks not at irrelevant noise. His neck is high,
subtle head, short belly and stout back,   80
his bold chest heaves with muscles. Good

spadices glaucique, color deterrimus albis
et gilvo. tum, si qua sonum procul arma dedere
stare loco nescit, micat auribus et tremit artus
collectumque premens volvit sub naribus ignem.
densa iuba, et dextro iactata recumbit in armo;
at duplex agitur per lumbos spina, cavatque
tellurem et solido graviter sonat ungula cornu.
talis Amyclaei domitus Pollucis habenis
90 Cyllarus et, quorum Grai meminere poetae,
Martis equi biiuges et magni currus Achilli.
talis et ipse iubam cervice effundit equina
coniugis adventu pernix Saturnus, et altum
Pelion hinnitu fugiens implevit acuto.

Hunc quoque, ubi aut morbo gravis aut iam segnior annis
deficit, abde domo, nec turpi ignosce senectae.
frigidus in Venerem senior, frustraque laborem
ingratum trahit, et, si quando ad proelia ventum est,
ut quondam in stipulis magnus sine viribus ignis,
100 incassum furit. ergo animos aevumque notabis
praecipue; hinc alias artis prolemque parentum
et quis cuique dolor victo, quae gloria palmae.
nonne vides, cum praecipiti certamine campum
corripuere ruuntque effusi carcere currus,
cum spes arrectae iuvenum, exsultantiaque haurit
corda pavor pulsans? illi instant verbere torto
et proni dant lora, volat vi fervidus axis;
iamque humiles, iamque elati sublime videntur
aëra per vacuum ferri atque adsurgere in auras;
110 nec mora nec requies; at fulvae nimbus harenae
tollitur, umescunt spumis flatuque sequentum:
tantus amor laudum, tantae est victoria curae.
primus Erichthonius currus et quattuor ausus

are bays and greys, worst colours white
and palomino. And again, at any far-off clash of arms
he can't stand still: he flicks his ears and quivers through
    his limbs
and snorting rolls from his nostrils gathering fire.
Thick his mane, and tossed cascades upon his right
    shoulder.
A double spinal ridge runs to his loins, his hoof
.gouges the dirt and heavy rings with solid horn.
Such was Cyllarus, broken by the bridle of Spartan Pollux,
and the yoked steeds of Mars, whom Greek poets   90
memorialize, and the mighty team of Achilles.
Such too, flinging his horse's mane across his withers
at his wife's approach, swift Saturn was, who filled
alpine Pelion with his shrill neigh as he fled.

Yet even such a horse, when burdened by disease or
    slowing with years
he fails, lock in the barn, and pity not the disgrace of age.
Older, cold his lust, and fruitlessly the joyless task
he drudges, and whenever it comes to skirmishing –
as sometimes through stubble a great impotent blaze –
he inflames in vain. So mettle and age you must mark   100
above all, then other points: the pedigree of parents,
what pangs each has in defeat, what pride in victory.
Don't you see, when in breakneck contest chariots rush
the field, and dash pouring from the gate,
when hope is steep for the young drivers and pounding
    panic drains
the bounding heart? They urge with whip twirling
and leaning slack the reins, the sparking axle fervent flies,
now low, now bounced aloft they seem
to push through empty atmosphere and mount the wind,
no flagging nor rest, but golden a cloud of sand's   110
flung up. They drip with foam and the pant of those
    pursuing:
so great their love of ovation, so great their zeal for victory.
Erichthonius first made bold to yoke four horses

iungere equos rapidusque rotis insistere victor.
frena Pelethronii Lapithae gyrosque dedere
impositi dorso, atque equitem docuere sub armis
insultare solo et gressus glomerare superbos.
aequus uterque labor, aeque iuvenemque magistri
exquirunt calidumque animis et cursibus acrem;
120   quamvis saepe fuga versos ille egerit hostis
et patriam Epirum referat fortisque Mycenas,
Neptunique ipsa deducat origine gentem.

His animadversis instant sub tempus et omnis
impendunt curas denso distendere pingui
quem legere ducem et pecori dixere maritum;
florentisque secant herbas fluviosque ministrant
farraque, ne blando nequeat superesse labori
invalidique patrum referant ieiunia nati.
ipsa autem macie tenuant armenta volentes,
130   atque, ubi concubitus primos iam nota voluptas
sollicitat, frondesque negant et fontibus arcent.
saepe etiam cursu quatiunt et sole fatigant,
cum graviter tunsis gemit area frugibus, et cum
surgentem ad Zephyrum paleae iactantur inanes.
hoc faciunt, nimio ne luxu obtunsior usus
sit genitali arvo et sulcos oblimet inertis,
sed rapiat sitiens Venerem interiusque recondat.

Rursus cura patrum cadere et succedere matrum
incipit. exactis gravidae cum mensibus errant,

to a chariot, to charge upright, victorious, swift above the
    wheels.
Horseback the Pelethronic Lapiths handed down manège,
the bridle and wheeling manoeuvres, and taught the armed
    cavalier
to vault across the earth, to round their haughty gait.
Equal each task, and equally the trainers seek a youth
hot in spirits and sharp in the races,
though often in retreating flight an elder steed may have
    chased the foe,   120
and claims his birthplace in Epirus or bold Mycenae
and from Neptune's own wellspring draws his bloodline.

These things considered, they work hard as the season
    nears,
apply all pains to bulk with thick fat
whom they have chosen leader and anointed husband of
    the herd.
Flowering herbs they cut, and serve him freshets
and spelt-meal, lest he be unequipped to meet the alluring
    toil,
lest flaccid foals repeat their scrawny sire.
But mares they starve to leanness wittingly,
and when first the instinctive pleasure flusters   130
them to sex, the trainers deny herbage and bar them from
    the springs.
Often too to galloping they goad them, and weary them
    with sun
when heavy the threshing-floor groans beneath corn and
    flail,
when upon the rising Zephyr the empty hulls are tossed.
This they do lest by much luxury the uterine soil's utility
be dulled, her furrow muddied to torpor,
but may clutch thirsting at the climax and garner it within.

By turns, the care of sires starts to wane, the care of dams
to wax. When, their months accomplished, swag-bellied
    they range

140   non illas gravibus quisquam iuga ducere plaustris,
      non saltu superare viam sit passus et acri
      carpere prata fuga fluviosque innare rapacis.
      saltibus in vacuis pascunt et plena secundum
      flumina, muscus ubi et viridissima gramine ripa,
      speluncaeque tegant et saxea procubet umbra.
      est lucos Silari circa ilicibusque virentem
      plurimus Alburnum volitans, cui nomen asilo
      Romanum est, oestrum Grai vertere vocantes,
      asper, acerba sonans, quo tota exterrita silvis
150   diffugiunt armenta; furit mugitibus aether
      concussus silvaeque et sicci ripa Tanagri.
      hoc quondam monstro horribilis exercuit iras
      Inachiae Iuno pestem meditata iuvencae.
      hunc quoque (nam mediis fervoribus acrior instat)
      arcebis gravido pecori, armentaque pasces
      sole recens orto aut noctem ducentibus astris.

      Post partum cura in vitulos traducitur omnis;
      continuoque notas et nomina gentis inurunt,
      et quos aut pecori malint submittere habendo
160   aut aris servare sacros aut scindere terram
      et campum horrentem fractis invertere glaebis.
      cetera pascuntur viridis armenta per herbas.
      tu quos ad studium atque usum formabis agrestem,
      iam vitulos hortare viamque insiste domandi,
      dum faciles animi iuvenum, dum mobilis aetas.
      ac primum laxos tenui de vimine circlos
      cervici subnecte; dehinc, ubi libera colla
      servitio adsuerint, ipsis e torquibus aptos
      iunge pares, et coge gradum conferre iuvencos;

let no one allow them in yoke to drag heavy carts,   140
or leaping to pass their way, or at a brisk gallop
to devour the meadow's breadth, or to swim in eddying
    streams.
In open glades the herdsmen graze them, and along the
    ` brimming
river, where moss grows and greenest banks of grass,
where coves may shelter, and rock-shadows may stretch.
There is among the Silaran woods and greened holms
of Alburnus a swarming fly, whose Roman name
is *asilus*, called *oestrus* in the evolving Greek,
aggressive, shrilly buzzing, before whom terrified
the whole herd stampedes the forest: the shocked ether
    crazes   150
at their bellowings, and the woods, and the droughted
    banks of the Tanager.
With this monster Juno once worked her dreadful wrath,
who hatched a plague for Inachus' daughter, heifered Io.
This too (for under sultry noon more fierce its torment)
you must fend from the pregnant flock, and pasture the
    herd
with the sun fresh up or when stars lead down the night.

After calving every care devolves upon the calves.
Straightway the stockmen sear them with a brand and
    mark their caste:
those they want to rear for the herd's sustaining,
those to keep sacred for the altars, those to tear the soil   160
and busting clods to upturn the ragged fields.
The other cattle are grazed among green grasses.
Those you would mould for pluck and rustic work
coax while yet calves, and enter in the way of training
while pliant their young spirits, while nimble their age.
First, slack loops of slender willow tie
around their necks. Then, when their freeborn necks
get used to servitude, yoke them in pairs
from those same halters fastened, and urge the steers keep
    step together;

170   atque illis iam saepe rotae ducantur inanes
       per terram, et summo vestigia pulvere signent;
       post valido nitens sub pondere faginus axis
       instrepat, et iunctos temo trahat aereus orbes.
       interea pubi indomitae non gramina tantum
       nec vescas salicum frondes ulvamque palustrem,
       sed frumenta manu carpes sata; nec tibi fetae
       more patrum nivea implebunt mulctraria vaccae,
       sed tota in dulcis consument ubera natos.

       Sin ad bella magis studium turmasque ferocis,
180   aut Alphea rotis praelabi flumina Pisae
       et Iovis in luco currus agitare volantis:
       primus equi labor est, animos atque arma videre
       bellantum lituosque pati, tractuque gementem
       ferre rotam et stabulo frenos audire sonantis;
       tum magis atque magis blandis gaudere magistri
       laudibus et plausae sonitum cervicis amare.
       atque haec iam primo depulsus ab ubere matris
       audeat, inque vicem det mollibus ora capistris
       invalidus etiamque tremens, etiam inscius aevi.
190   at tribus exactis ubi quarta accesserit aestas,
       carpere mox gyrum incipiat gradibusque sonare
       compositis, sinuetque alterna volumina crurum,
       sitque laboranti similis; tum cursibus auras,
       tum vocet, ac per aperta volans ceu liber habenis
       aequora vix summa vestigia ponat harena,
       qualis Hyperboreis Aquilo cum densus ab oris
       incubuit, Scythiaeque hiemes atque arida differt
       nubila; tum segetes altae campique natantes
       lenibus horrescunt flabris, summaeque sonorem
200   dant silvae longique urgent ad litora fluctus;

and often now let loadless carts be dragged by them   170
across the land, grooving only the topmost dust.
Later beneath a rugged weight let the greased beech axle
creak, and a bronzed hitchpole drag the wheels.
Meanwhile give their untamed youth not just meadowgrass
nor half-browsed willow leaves and marshy sedge
but hand-plucked grain. Your brood cows will not
brim their snowy milk-pails in the custom of our fathers
but all their udder squander on their darling calves.

But if for war you hanker more, for squadrons brave,
or to glide on wheels beside Pisa's River Alpheus,   180
through Jovan groves to drive the chariot to flight . . .
The horse's first task is to witness the nerve
and weaponry of warriors, to endure the clarion, to
        stomach the groan
of the dragged wheel, and in the stall to hear bits jangling,
then more and more to thrill at the honeyed praises of the
        trainer,
to love the sound of his own neck patted.
All this let him tackle as soon as he's weaned from his
        mother's teat,
and bit by bit let him tender his mouth to soft halters
while weak and trembling still, still green in years.
But when, three summers passed, the fourth draws nigh,   190
let him start to storm around the training course, to ring
        his paces
evenly, and let him bow the alternating flexion of his legs:
let him be as exertion's self. Then let him challenge
the wind to laps, and over the exposed flats flying, as
        unreined,
barely set his hoofprint in the surface sand.
As when from Hyperborean coasts the clenched north wind
hammers down, shoving Scythian frosts before it
and rainless clouds, then tall wheatfields and the marine
        plain
ripple in the gentle gusts, the treetops rustle and long
toward the shoreline rollers press,   200

ille volat simul arva fuga simul aequora verrens.
hinc vel ad Elei metas et maxima campi
sudabit spatia et spumas aget ore cruentas,
Belgica vel molli melius feret esseda collo.
tum demum crassa magnum farragine corpus
crescere iam domitis sinito: namque ante domandum
ingentis tollent animos, prensique negabunt
verbera lenta pati et duris parere lupatis.

Sed non ulla magis viris industria firmat,
210 quam Venerem et caeci stimulos avertere amoris,
sive boum sive est cui gratior usus equorum.
atque ideo tauros procul atque in sola relegant
pascua post montem oppositum et trans flumina lata,
aut intus clausos satura ad praesepia servant.
carpit enim viris paulatim uritque videndo
femina, nec nemorum patitur meminisse nec herbae
dulcibus illa quidem inlecebris, et saepe superbos
cornibus inter se subigit decernere amantis.
pascitur in magna Sila formosa iuvenca:
220 illi alternantes multa vi proelia miscent
volneribus crebris, lavit ater corpora sanguis,
versaque in obnixos urguentur cornua vasto
cum gemitu; reboant silvaeque et longus Olympus.
nec mos bellantis una stabulare, sed alter
victus abit longeque ignotis exsulat oris,
multa gemens ignominiam plagasque superbi
victoris, tum quos amisit inultus amores,
et stabula aspectans regnis excessit avitis.

and on it soars, swift, sweeping soil and seas the same.
A horse like that will sweat the vast courses of the plain
toward the finish posts at Elis, and blow bloody foam
    from his mouth,
or will bear the Belgian chariot more bravely, steady of
    neck.
At last with thick mash let their bodies plump
after they've been broken in – before their breaking,
immoderate they rouse their spunk, and lassoed they scorn
to truckle to the limber lash, to heed the jagged bit.

But whether handling cows or horses suits you better
no diligence steels their sinew more
than to prevent desire and the pricks of blinding love.   210
Therefore to solitary pastures far removed handlers banish
the bull, beyond a mountain obstacle, across rivers broad,
or keep him locked inside a well-stocked stall.
For the female, when he sees her, stokes him up and
    winnows by degrees
his strength, nor does she with her fetching lures
permit him even to recall groves or meadows, and often
    whets
her lordly lovers to settle things among themselves with
    horns.
She grazes Sila's hightop, gorgeous heifer:
her suitors taking turns with greatest vehemence join
    battle   220
in frequent wounds, black blood bathes their bodies,
bent horns rammed against the rival's defiance
with a ragged bellow, and wide the woods and sky bellow
    back.
Nor tend the rivals to stable together, but the one
bested slinks off and distant dwells an exile in unfamiliar
    climes,
loudly lamenting his disgrace and the blows of his boastful
victor, and what loves he's lost unavenged:
glancing back at his stall, he passes from his ancestral
    realm.

ergo omni cura viris exercet et inter
230   dura iacet pernix instrato saxa cubili
frondibus hirsutis et carice pastus acuta,
et temptat sese atque irasci in cornua discit
arboris obnixus trunco, ventosque lacessit
ictibus, et sparsa ad pugnam proludit harena.
post ubi collectum robur viresque refectae,
signa movet praecepsque oblitum fertur in hostem:
fluctus uti medio coepit cum albescere ponto,
longius ex altoque sinum trahit, utque volutus
ad terras immane sonat per saxa, neque ipso
240   monte minor procumbit; at ima exaestuat unda
verticibus nigramque alte subiectat harenam.

Omne adeo genus in terris hominumque ferarumque,
et genus aequoreum, pecudes pictaeque volucres,
in furias ignemque ruunt: amor omnibus idem.
tempore non alio catulorum oblita leaena
saevior erravit campis, nec funera volgo
tam multa informes ursi stragemque dedere
per silvas; tum saevus aper, tum pessima tigris;
heu male tum Libyae solis erratur in agris.
250   nonne vides, ut tota tremor pertemptet equorum
corpora, si tantum notas odor attulit auras?
ac neque eos iam frena virum neque verbera saeva,
non scopuli rupesque cavae atque obiecta retardant
flumina correptosque unda torquentia montis.
ipse ruit dentesque Sabellicus exacuit sus,
et pede prosubigit terram, fricat arbore costas
atque hinc atque illinc umeros ad volnera durat.
quid iuvenis, magnum cui versat in ossibus ignem
durus amor? nempe abruptis turbata procellis
260   nocte natat caeca serus freta; quem super ingens

So now with all vigilance his strength he trains, and lies
nightlong among rugged stones on an unpetalled bed   230
with nettled leaves and thorny sedge for forage,
and tests himself, and learns to rage through his horns,
lunging at a tree trunk, challenging the wind
with jabs, kicking up sand in practice for the brawl.
Later, when his pith is mustered and his strength recovered
he takes up his banner and headlong charges his oblivious
        foe:
as when a wave begins to whiten in mid-sea
and further from the deep winds up its curl, and rolling
shoreward wildly booms through the shingle, a veritable
mountain, not crashing flat but its deepest surge boils up   240
in whorls and sprays black sand skyward.

Indeed, all species on the earth, both man and beast,
the kingdom undersea, cattle and painted birds
into this hot lunacy rush: love strikes all the same.
In no season else the lioness ignoring her cubs
more savagely roams the veldt, nor deals the misshapen
bear so much murder, so much havoc, so wildly
through the forest; then the boar's amok, then the tigress
        most a hellcat.
O how dire then to wander Libya's solitary fields!
Do you not see how a shudder runs all through the
        stallions'   250
flesh, if scarcely the scent brings them familiar musks?
Now neither men's bits nor the furious scourge
curb them, no crags nor sloughed-out bluffs stay them, nor
        rivers
which snatch up and pitch mountains with their rushing.
The Sabine boar tears around, hones his tusks,
and with his hoof paws up dirt, rubs his flanks against a
        tree,
roughens his shoulders this side and that against wounds.
What does that young buck, in whose bones a lusty flame
cruel love stokes? Why, in the chaos of jolting storms
he swims the straits in the blind night. Above him   260

porta tonat caeli, et scopulis inlisa reclamant
aequora; nec miseri possunt revocare parentes,
nec moritura super crudeli funere virgo.
quid lynces Bacchi variae et genus acre luporum
atque canum? quid quae imbelles dant proelia cervi?
scilicet ante omnis furor est insignis equarum;
et mentem Venus ipsa dedit, quo tempore Glauci
Potniades malis membra absumpsere quadrigae.
illas ducit amor trans Gargara transque sonantem
270 Ascanium; superant montis et flumina tranant.
continuoque avidis ubi subdita flamma medullis
(vere magis, quia vere calor redit ossibus), illae
ore omnes versae in Zephyrum stant rupibus altis,
exceptantque levis auras, et saepe sine ullis
coniugiis vento gravidae (mirabile dictu)
saxa per et scopulos et depressas convallis
diffugiunt, non, Eure, tuos, neque solis ad ortus,
in Borean Caurumque, aut unde nigerrimus Auster
nascitur et pluvio contristat frigore caelum.
280 hic demum, hippomanes vero quod nomine dicunt
pastores, lentum destillat ab inguine virus,
hippomanes, quod saepe malae legere novercae
miscueruntque herbas et non innoxia verba.

Sed fugit interea, fugit inreparabile tempus,
singula dum capti circumvectamur amore.
hoc satis armentis: superat pars altera curae,
lanigeros agitare greges hirtasque capellas.

thunders heaven's mighty gate, and pounding on the
    headland
the sea responds; nor can his doleful parents call him back,
nor the virgin who in cruel ruin must die too.
What of Bacchus' spotted lynxes and the fanged race of
    wolves
and dogs? what of the battles which else-peaceable stags
    wage?
But O, the mares' madness more flagrant than all:
Venus herself dowered them this passion, on the day the
    four Potnian
race-mares devoured with their chops the limbs of Glaucus.
Love drives them over Gargara, across the roaring
Ascanius, they traverse mountains and swim rivers.   270
Just when into their insatiable hearts the flame's insinuated
(and more in spring, for in spring heat returns to their
    bosoms), they all
with mouths angled to the west winds stand on steepy cliffs
and swallow the mild breezes, and often, without any
    marriage
pregnant by the wind (strange to say!)
they scuttle through rocks and through badlands, through
    low vales –
not, O eastwind, toward yours or the sun's rising
but to north and north-west, or whither blackest
    southwinds
spawn and gloom the sky with chilling rain.
Then at last, the *hippomanes* – aptly shepherds call it   280
by that name, 'horse-madness': its viscous slime
drips from the groin, which often wicked stepmothers
    collect,
brewing up herbs with malevolent spells.

Meanwhile it flies, time flies irretrievably,
while captivated with love we ramble through minutiae.
Here's enough of herds. There remains the other part of my
    work:
to attend the lanate flocks and shaggy goats.

hic labor, hinc laudem fortes sperate coloni.
nec sum animi dubius, verbis ea vincere magnum
290 quam sit et angustis hunc addere rebus honorem;
sed me Parnasi deserta per ardua dulcis
raptat amor; iuvat ire iugis, qua nulla priorum
Castaliam molli devertitur orbita clivo.
nunc, veneranda Pales, magno nunc ore sonandum.

Incipiens stabulis edico in mollibus herbam
carpere ovis, dum mox frondosa reducitur aestas,
et multa duram stipula filicumque maniplis
sternere subter humum, glacies ne frigida laedat
molle pecus scabiemque ferat turpisque podagras.
300 post hinc digressus iubeo frondentia capris
arbuta sufficere et fluvios praebere recentis,
et stabula a ventis hiberno opponere soli
ad medium conversa diem, cum frigidus olim
iam cadit extremoque inrorat Aquarius anno.
haec quoque non cura nobis leviore tuendae,
nec minor usus erit, quamvis Milesia magno
vellera mutentur Tyrios incocta rubores.
densior hinc suboles, hinc largi copia lactis;
quam magis exhausto spumaverit ubere mulctra,
310 laeta magis pressis manabunt flumina mammis.
nec minus interea barbas incanaque menta
Cinyphii tondent hirci saetasque comantis
usum in castrorum et miseris velamina nautis.
pascuntur vero silvas et summa Lycaei
horrentisque rubos et amantis ardua dumos;
atque ipsae memores redeunt in tecta suosque
ducunt et gravido superant vix ubere limen.
ergo omni studio glaciem ventosque nivalis
quo minor est illis curae mortalis egestas,

Here is labour, here hope for glory, hale husbandmen.
I know how hard it is to prevail with words to greatness
in such things, to pile honour onto slight stuff;   290
but through the craggy wilds of Parnassus sweet love
yanks me. What joy to run over ridges where no forerunner
    rut
winds a gentle slope down to Castalia!
Now, revered Pales, now with lofty tongue must we
    declaim.

First, I proclaim that sheep should graze their fodder
in cushy cotes, until shortly summer is squired in, beleaved,
and that you strow with straw and handfuls of fern
the hard dirt beneath them, lest freezing ice shock
the tender flock, bringing scabies and gruesome foot rot.
Next, I enjoin you to supply leafy arbutes   300
to the goats, and to offer fresh streams,
and to position their stalls away from the wind, toward
the winter sun in its slanting southern noon, when cold
Aquarius is setting, sprinkling the year's horizon.
These nannies too we must tend with no less care –
nor less will be the profit, though Milesian wools
are traded dear, steeped in Tyrian purple.
But here's more frequent young, hence lavish the supply of
    milk:
the more the milk-pail froths beneath the squeezed-out
    teat,
the more richly from the squeezed-out teat will spurt the
    stream.   310
Moreover, men clip the beard on the Cinyphian goat's
greyed chin, and shave his shaggy bristles
for use as tarps in bivouacs and for careworn mariners.
Plus, they browse the woods and heights of Lycaeus
on thorned brambles and cliff-loving brake,
and of themselves are mindful to return to their stalls, kids
in tow, and scarcely clear the threshold with full udders.
Therefore, the less their mortal need for care, the more
with zeal from ice and wintry winds preserve them,

320   avertes, victumque feres et virgea laetus
         pabula, nec tota claudes faenilia bruma.

         At vero Zephyris cum laeta vocantibus aestas
         in saltus utrumque gregem atque in pascua mittet,
         Luciferi primo cum sidere frigida rura
         carpamus, dum mane novum, dum gramina canent,
         et ros in tenera pecori gratissimus herba.
         inde ubi quarta sitim caeli collegerit hora
         et cantu querulae rumpent arbusta cicadae,
         ad puteos aut alta greges ad stagna iubebo
330   currentem ilignis potare canalibus undam;
         aestibus at mediis umbrosam exquirere vallem,
         sicubi magna Iovis antiquo robore quercus
         ingentis tendat ramos, aut sicubi nigrum
         ilicibus crebris sacra nemus accubet umbra;
         tum tenuis dare rursus aquas et pascere rursus
         solis ad occasum, cum frigidus aëra Vesper
         temperat, et saltus reficit iam roscida luna
         litoraque alcyonem resonant, acalanthida dumi.

         Quid tibi pastores Libyae, quid pascua versu
340   prosequar et raris habitata mapalia tectis?
         saepe diem noctemque et totum ex ordine mensem
         pascitur itque pecus longa in deserta sine ullis
         hospitiis: tantum campi iacet. omnia secum
         armentarius Afer agit, tectumque laremque
         armaque Amyclaeumque canem Cressamque pharetram;
         non secus ac patriis acer Romanus in armis
         iniusto sub fasce viam cum carpit, et hosti
         ante exspectatum positis stat in agmine castris.

                                    *

bring provision and twiggy feed with cheer,   320
nor shut your haylofts up all winter long.

But sure, when at the Zephyr's summons bright summer
sends sheep and goats into clearings and pastures,
at the morning star's first light let us take to the cool
meadows, while morning's new, while grasses pale,
while dew upon the tender green most cordial to the flocks.
Then when the fourth hour of the sky has built their thirst
and with plaints the fretful cicadas shatter the woodlands,
beside wells and beside deep pools I'll bid the flocks
to drink the water rushing in oaken gutters,   330
in midday heat to seek a shady swale,
wherever with its ancient strength the mighty oak of Jove
spreads spacious branches, or wherever dark
with holm oaks lush the grove lounges in holy shade.
Then offer again the trickling water and graze them again
to sunset, when cool the evening star soothes the air
and the moon bedewed refreshes the thickets,
when the frith cries with the kingfisher, the furze with finch.

Why Libyan shepherds, why their pastures should I trace
     for you
in verse, their stockyards squatted with sparse gourbi-
     huts?   340
Over and over day and night and through a whole month
     unbroken
their flocks graze and range in godforsaken deserts
with nary a friendly roof, so vast the waste sprawls. Along
     with him
the African herdsman carries everything, his house and
     hearth
and arms and Spartan dogs and Cretan quiver:
just like the bold Roman in his homeland's arms,
when he picks his way beneath his oppressive kit, and
     before
the enemy anticipates him halts with his troop to pitch camp.

*

At non, qua Scythiae gentes Maeotiaque unda,
350 turbidus et torquens flaventis Hister harenas,
quaque redit medium Rhodope porrecta sub axem.
illic clausa tenent stabulis armenta, neque ullae
aut herbae campo apparent aut arbore frondes;
sed iacet aggeribus niveis informis et alto
terra gelu late septemque adsurgit in ulnas.
semper hiems, semper spirantes frigora Cauri.
tum Sol pallentis haud umquam discutit umbras,
nec cum invectus equis altum petit aethera, nec cum
praecipitem Oceani rubro lavit aequore currum.
360 concrescunt subitae currenti in flumine crustae,
undaque iam tergo ferratos sustinet orbis,
puppibus illa prius, patulis nunc hospita plaustris;
aeraque dissiliunt volgo, vestesque rigescunt
indutae, caeduntque securibus umida vina,
et totae solidam in glaciem vertere lacunae,
stiriaque impexis induruit horrida barbis.
interea toto non setius aëre ninguit:
intereunt pecudes, stant circumfusa pruinis
corpora magna boum, confertoque agmine cervi
370 torpent mole nova et summis vix cornibus exstant.
hos non immissis canibus, non cassibus ullis
puniceaeve agitant pavidos formidine pinnae,
sed frustra oppositum trudentis pectore montem
comminus obtruncant ferro graviterque rudentis
caedunt et magno laeti clamore reportant.
ipsi in defossis specubus secura sub alta
otia agunt terra, congestaque robora totasque

How diffcrent there, where Scythian tribes, where Lake
    Maeotis lies,
and tousled the Danube spins its golden sands,   350
where Rhodope bends stretching toward the central pole.
There penned in stalls they keep their herds, and no
green shows upon the steppe nor leaves in the trees,
but wide the earth slumps lumpen under mounds of snow
and mounts in deep ice seven cubits high.
Always winter, always the frosty wheezings of the
    northwind.
And the sun never dissipates the pale haze,
not when borne behind his steeds he steers for heaven's
    zenith, nor
when he splashes his breakneck chariot into Ocean's
    reddened scape.
Sudden ice crusts cluster upon the brisk beck   360
and soon the water hcfts the iron-clad wheel on its back –
once ships, now bulky wagons welcoming.
Brass buckles everywhere, clothes freeze
upon the back, they chop with hatchets their liquid wine,
whole ponds into solid ice transform,
and the jagged icicle glazes upon the uncombed beard.
Meanwhile, no less, the sky entire is snowing:
the cattle perish, shrouded in frost, the bulls
in their massive girth stock-still, and in a packed herd the
    deer
numb beneath the unaccustomed flurry and barely poke
    antler-tips out.   370
These the Scythians hunt not with hounds unleashed, nor
    any snares,
nor by spooking with strands of red feathers,
but as they strive vainly to breast the mountain front
men butcher them with short-axes, hack them down
amid heavy bawlings, and with great whoops exultant bear
    them home.
The men themselves, in dug-out caves carefree and deep in
    earth
enjoy peace, rolling to the firepit whole elms,

advolvere focis ulmos ignique dedere.
hic noctem ludo ducunt, et pocula laeti
380 fermento atque acidis imitantur vitea sorbis.
talis Hyperboreo septem subiecta trioni
gens effrena virum Rhipaeo tunditur Euro
et pecudum fulvis velatur corpora saetis.

Si tibi lanitium curae, primum aspera silva
lappaeque tribolique absint; fuge pabula laeta,
continuoque greges villis lege mollibus albos.
illum autem, quamvis aries sit candidus ipse,
nigra subest udo tantum cui lingua palato,
reice, ne maculis infuscet vellera pullis
390 nascentum, plenoque alium circumspice campo.
munere sic niveo lanae, si credere dignum est,
Pan deus Arcadiae captam te, Luna, fefellit
in nemora alta vocans; nec tu aspernata vocantem.

At cui lactis amor, cytisum lotosque frequentis
ipse manu salsasque ferat praesepibus herbas.
hinc et amant fluvios magis, et magis ubera tendunt
et salis occultum referunt in lacte saporem.
multi etiam excretos prohibent a matribus haedos,
primaque ferratis praefigunt ora capistris.
400 quod surgente die mulsere horisque diurnis,
nocte premunt; quod iam tenebris et sole cadente,
sub lucem exportant calathis (adit oppida pastor);
aut parco sale contingunt hiemique reponunt.

Nec tibi cura canum fuerit postrema, sed una
velocis Spartae catulos acremque Molossum
pasce sero pingui. numquam custodibus illis
nocturnum stabulis furem incursusque luporum

heaped-up trunks, committing them to the blaze.
Here they spool out the night with play, and merry they
    pretend
cups of wine by barming sour service-berries.   380
Such is this race of men unbridled, Hyperborean, pitched
beneath the Bear's seven stars, buffeted by Rhipaean
    easterlies,
their bodies bundled in the tawny pelts of beasts.

If your concern is wool, first the snagging scrub
of burrs and thistles cut away, shun rich pastures
and at the start select white sheep with downy fleece.
But that ram, however dazzling white he be,
whose tongue lies black beneath his drooling palate
drive out, lest with spots he sully the wool of newborn
    lambs:
look around for another in your well-stocked yard.   390
With the white gift of such wool, if it's worth believing,
Pan the god of Arcadia beguiled you, charmed Luna,
into secluded bowers calling you – nor did you spurn his
    call.

But let him who loves milk fetch to the stalls
lotus and clover by his own hand, and salted feed,
whence they crave streams the more, and more their udders
    swell,
and in their milk retain a sneaking smack of salt.
Many even keep the kids corralled from their nannies
and from the first with iron muzzles cap their mouths.
What they milk at daybreak or in daylight hours   400
at night they press, and what at sunset or at night they milk
at first light carry off in baskets (if to town a goatherd go),
or touch it with scant salt and lay it in for winter.

Nor should your least care be the care of dogs, but feed
swift Spartan pups and fierce Molossians the same
on fattening whey. Never, these guard-dogs at the stables,
will you fear the midnight rustler, or raid of wolves,

aut impacatos a tergo horrebis Hiberos.
saepe etiam cursu timidos agitabis onagros,
410 et canibus leporem, canibus venabere dammas;
saepe volutabris pulsos silvestribus apros
latratu turbabis agens, montisque per altos
ingentem clamore premes ad retia cervum.

Disce et odoratam stabulis accendere cedrum
galbaneoque agitare gravis nidore chelydros.
saepe sub immotis praesepibus aut mala tactu
vipera delituit caelumque exterrita fugit,
aut tecto adsuetus coluber succedere et umbrae
(pestis acerba boum) pecorique aspergere virus,
420 fovit humum. cape saxa manu, cape robora, pastor,
tollentemque minas et sibila colla tumentem
deice. iamque fuga timidum caput abdidit alte,
cum medii nexus extremaeque agmina caudae
solvuntur, tardosque trahit sinus ultimus orbis.
est etiam ille malus Calabris in saltibus anguis,
squamea convolvens sublato pectore terga
atque notis longam maculosus grandibus alvum,
qui, dum amnes ulli rumpuntur fontibus et dum
vere madent udo terrae ac pluvialibus Austris,
430 stagna colit, ripisque habitans hic piscibus atram
improbus ingluviem ranisque loquacibus explet;
postquam exusta palus, terraeque ardore dehiscunt,
exsilit in siccum, et flammantia lumina torquens
saevit agris asperque siti atque exterritus aestu.
ne mihi tum mollis sub divo carpere somnos
neu dorso nemoris libeat iacuisse per herbas,

or restless banditos skulking round the rear.
And often will you coursing chase the startled ass
and hares with hounds, and with hounds hunt the doe.   410
Often from their woodland wallows will you roust boars,
driving them with barking, and with howls across the
    mountaintop
force a giant stag into your nets.

Learn to smudge your stalls with fragrant cedar,
with fennel smoke to rout out noisome water-snakes.
Often beneath unscoured cribs the viper lurks,
death to touch, recoiling from the sun uneasy,
or else an adder – prone to climb into the roof and from its
    shelter
(bitter plague of oxen) sprinkle venom on the cattle –
hugs the ground. Grab stones in hand, grab cudgels,
    shepherd,   420
and as he coils up his threats and puffs his hissing neck,
clobber him. Now in flight, low he ducks his cowered head
while the twines of his guts and his trailing tail-tip
unwind, and the last coil drags its slow knots.
And then there's that dire serpent in Calabrian dells,
twisting her scaly back with upreared breast
and streaked with big splotches on her long belly,
who – while any streams yet jet from their fountainhead,
while the earth oozes under spring humours or stormy
    southwinds –
works the pool, and holing up on shore implacable   430
she crams her venom-black maw with fish and chattering
    frogs.
Later when the marshland's parched, when the soil gapes
    with heat,
she dives onto dry land, and rolling her fiery glare
furies through the fields savage with thirst and panicked by
    the heat.
O let me not seek to woo soft sleep beneath an open sky
nor to loll among the grasses along a timbered ridge

cum positis novus exuviis nitidusque iuventa
volvitur, aut catulos tectis aut ova relinquens,
arduus ad solem et linguis micat ore trisulcis.

440   Morborum quoque te causas et signa docebo.
turpis ovis temptat scabies, ubi frigidus imber
altius ad vivum persedit et horrida cano
bruma gelu, vel cum tonsis inlotus adhaesit
sudor, et hirsuti secuerunt corpora vepres.
dulcibus idcirco fluviis pecus omne magistri
perfundunt, udisque aries in gurgite villis
mersatur, missusque secundo defluit amni;
aut tonsum tristi contingunt corpus amurca,
et spumas miscent argenti vivaque sulpura

450   Idaeasque pices et pinguis unguine ceras
scillamque elleborosque gravis nigrumque bitumen.
non tamen ulla magis praesens fortuna laborum est,
quam si quis ferro potuit rescindere summum
ulceris os: alitur vitium vivitque tegendo,
dum medicas adhibere manus ad volnera pastor
abnegat, et meliora deos sedet omnia poscens.
quin etiam, ima dolor balantum lapsus ad ossa
cum furit atque artus depascitur arida febris,
profuit incensos aestus avertere et inter

460   ima ferire pedis salientem sanguine venam,
Bisaltae quo more solent acerque Gelonus,
cum fugit in Rhodopen atque in deserta Getarum
et lac concretum cum sanguine potat equino.
quam procul aut molli succedere saepius umbrae
videris aut summas carpentem ignavius herbas
extremamque sequi, aut medio procumbere campo
pascentem, et serae solam decedere nocti,
continuo culpam ferro compesce, prius quam

when then, her moult sloughed off, fresh and sleek with
    youth
she winds, leaving hatchlings or eggs in her nest,
craning toward the sun, and flickering at the mouth with a
    three-forked tongue.

Of diseases too, their causes and signs, I will teach you.   440
Ugly scabies attacks the sheep when freezing rain
deep into the quick has soaked, and winter bristling with
    hoar frost,
or when sweat clings unwashed to their sheared hides
and pricking thorns gouge their flanks.
For this reason in sweet rivers herdsmen douse
the whole flock: the ram is dunked into the gurge
    unharnessed
and with fleeces soaked floats downstream.
Or they daub the sheared flesh with rank oil-lees,
mixing in silver slag and raw sulphur,
pitch from Ida and rich oily wax,   450
krill, pungent hellebore, and black tar.
Yet no succour is more timely for their suffering
than if one can with a blade slice open the pustule's
bulging head: corruption thrives and breeds covert,
while the shepherd holds off laying healing hands
upon the sores, sits tight, prays that the gods mend all.
What's more, when plunged to the inmost marrow the pain
maddens the bleating sheep and parched fever devours
    their joints,
it profits to turn away the raging heat, and to lance
the vein throbbing with blood within the hoof's cleft,   460
in the Macedonian's wonted style, and the bold Scyth's
as he speeds to Rhodope and the Thracian wastes
and swills milk curdled with horse blood.
If you should see one slipping far off into soft shade
or picking listlessly at grass-tips,
straggling behind, or stumbling in the middle of the pasture
at feed, retiring alone into the late night,
at once with your knife jugulate the infection, before

dira per incautum serpant contagia volgus.
470   non tam creber agens hiemem ruit aequore turbo,
quam multae pecudum pestes. nec singula morbi
corpora corripiunt, sed tota aestiva repente,
spemque gregemque simul cunctamque ab origine gentem.
tum sciat, aërias Alpis et Norica si quis
castella in tumulis et Iapydis arva Timavi
nunc quoque post tanto videat, desertaque regna
pastorum et longe saltus lateque vacantis.

Hic quondam morbo caeli miseranda coorta est
tempestas totoque autumni incanduit aestu,
480   et genus omne neci pecudum dedit, omne ferarum,
corrupitque lacus, infecit pabula tabo.
nec via mortis erat simplex; sed ubi ignea venis
omnibus acta sitis miseros adduxerat artus,
rursus abundabat fluidus liquor omniaque in se
ossa minutatim morbo conlapsa trahebat.
saepe in honore deum medio stans hostia ad aram,
lanea dum nivea circumdatur infula vitta,
inter cunctantis cecidit moribunda ministros.
aut si quam ferro mactaverat ante sacerdos,
490   inde neque impositis ardent altaria fibris,
nec responsa potest consultus reddere vates,
ac vix suppositi tinguntur sanguine cultri
summaque ieiuna sanie infuscatur harena.
hinc laetis vituli volgo moriuntur in herbis
et dulcis animas plena ad praesepia reddunt;

the contagion snakes dire through your unwary flock.
Not so rampant bursts the hurricane, driving squalls from
    open sea,   470
as pestilence infests cattle. Diseases seize
not single bodies but a whole summer's pasture at a blow,
the flock and its future together, the whole stock plucked at
    its roots.
You'd know this if you saw – even now, years later – the
    ethereal Alps,
the hilltop Noric keeps, the Illyrian fields of Timavus: still
    desolate
their shepherds' realms, far and wide their paddocks
    deserted.

Once from a sickness of sky there arose here a season
pitiable, when the whole of autumn glared white hot.
Each breed of cattle it sentenced to be slain, and all wild
    beasts.   480
It defiled the lakes, it putrefied the fodder with its poison.
Nor was the way to death unvarying, but when fiery
    through all the veins
thirst had coursed and withered their stricken shanks,
in turn a rheumy fluid bloated up, and seeped itself
into every bone mouldering cell by cell in disease.
Often in the middle of oblations for the gods, the victim
    waiting at the altar,
the woollen fillet with its snow-white garland circling its
    brow,
dropped dead among the dawdling ministrants.
Or even if, before it succumbed, the priest slaughtered with
    his blade,
neither did the altars blaze from the entrails laid upon,   490
nor could the oracle implored return an explanation.
Scarce the knife underthroat sheened with blood,
the sand darkened only surface-deep with the thin gore.
Then everywhere among lilting grasses the calves fall dead,
and give up their dear lives beside well-stocked mangers.

hinc canibus blandis rabies venit, et quatit aegros
tussis anhela sues ac faucibus angit obesis.
labitur infelix studiorum atque immemor herbae
victor equus fontisque avertitur et pede terram
500   crebra ferit; demissae aures, incertus ibidem
sudor et ille quidem morituris frigidus; aret
pellis et ad tactum tractanti dura resistit.
haec ante exitium primis dant signa diebus;
sin in processu coepit crudescere morbus,
tum vero ardentes oculi atque attractus ab alto
spiritus, interdum gemitu gravis, imaque longo
ilia singultu tendunt, it naribus ater
sanguis, et obsessas fauces premit aspera lingua.
profuit inserto latices infundere cornu
510   Lenaeos; ea visa salus morientibus una:
mox erat hoc ipsum exitio, furiisque refecti
ardebant, ipsique suos iam morte sub aegra
(di meliora piis erroremque hostibus illum!)
discissos nudis laniabant dentibus artus.
ecce autem duro fumans sub vomere taurus
concidit et mixtum spumis vomit ore cruorem
extremosque ciet gemitus. it tristis arator,
maerentem abiungens fraterna morte iuvencum,
atque opere in medio defixa relinquit aratra.
520   non umbrae altorum nemorum, non mollia possunt
prata movere animum, non qui per saxa volutus
purior electro campum petit amnis; at ima
solvuntur latera, atque oculos stupor urguet inertis
ad terramque fluit devexo pondere cervix.

Then upon the fawning dogs comes madness, and a rasping
      cough
shakes the weakening hogs and strangles them with their
      swollen gullets.
The triumphant stallion dwindles and fails; neglectful of his
      zeal
and of clover he turns from the springs and with frequent
pawings rakes the earth: drooped ears, which fitful   500
sweat – sweat that runs cold near dying. His hide
dries out, and hard beneath the hand resists handling.
Such signs they give in the first days before death.
But if in its advance the plague begins to fiercen,
then ah! – the blazing eyes, the wheeze racked up from deep
within, sometimes freighted with moaning, their inmost
      guts
wrenched with long sobs, black blood spurting
from the nostrils, and the ragged tongue chokes the
      blocked throat.
It *seemed* help to pour in wine-juice through a horn
in-crammed – it seemed the single balm for the dying . . .   510
but soon this too was for ruin, for refreshed in rage
they burned, and even under the droop of death
(God deal the pious better, and such madness to our
      enemies!)
with bared teeth mangled their own broken limbs.
And behold: the bull, steaming beneath the iron plough
collapses, and vomits from his mouth blood mixed with
      foam
and shudders his last groans. The ploughman trudges
      disconsolate,
unyokes the bullock mourning his brother's death
and abandons the plough wedged halfway through its
      work.
No shade of deep groves nor soft pastures   520
can stir his spirit, nor the river clearer than amber
among the rocks tumbling hard for the plain; but his flanks
utterly slack, and a stupor weighs his listless eyes,
his neck slumps to the ground with sagging weight.

quid labor aut benefacta iuvant? quid vomere terras
invertisse gravis? atqui non Massica Bacchi
munera, non illis epulae nocuere repostae:
frondibus et victu pascuntur simplicis herbae,
pocula sunt fontes liquidi atque exercita cursu
530 flumina, nec somnos abrumpit cura salubris.
tempore non alio dicunt regionibus illis
quaesitas ad sacra boves Iunonis et uris
imparibus ductos alta ad donaria currus.
ergo aegre rastris terram rimantur, et ipsis
unguibus infodiunt fruges, montisque per altos
contenta cervice trahunt stridentia plaustra.
non lupus insidias explorat ovilia circum
nec gregibus nocturnus obambulat; acrior illum
cura domat. timidi dammae cervique fugaces
540 nunc interque canes et circum tecta vagantur.
iam maris immensi prolem et genus omne natantum
litore in extremo ceu naufraga corpora fluctus
proluit; insolitae fugiunt in flumina phocae.
interit et curvis frustra defensa latebris
vipera et attoniti squamis adstantibus hydri.
ipsis est aër avibus non aequus, et illae
praecipites alta vitam sub nube relinquunt.
praeterea iam nec mutari pabula refert,
quaesitaeque nocent artes; cessere magistri,
550 Phillyrides Chiron Amythaoniusque Melampus.
saevit et in lucem Stygiis emissa tenebris
pallida Tisiphone Morbos agit ante Metumque,
inque dies avidum surgens caput altius effert.
balatu pecorum et crebris mugitibus amnes
arentesque sonant ripae collesque supini.
iamque catervatim dat stragem atque aggerat ipsis

What good his labour or his service? Why with the share
upturn the heavy soil? (And yet no Massic indulgence
from the vine has worked such harm to them, nor banquets
    spread:
they graze on leaves, on provender of simple grass,
their draughts are flowing springs and rivers lively
coursing, and no worry breaks their wholesome dreams!)   530
But at no other time, they say, were cattle rounded up
from the back-country for Juno's offerings, and the
    processional
drawn by oxen wild, outsized, to the exalted shrine.
Thus men claw the earth with arduous rakes, and with
    their own
fingernails drill in the seeds, and over the hilltops
with strained necks drag the creaking wagons.
The wolf scopes out no stratagems around the sheepfold,
nor nightly prowls the flocks; a sharper
care tames him. Timid stags and skittish does
now drift among the hounds and around the village.   540
The brood of the unfathomable sea, and all the race of
    swimmers
wash up along the shoreline like shipwrecked hulls upon
    the breakers,
and the prodigious seals flee up into rivers.
Now perishes the viper, unavailing his barricade in winding
lair, and the water-snake, stunned with scales bristling.
The air is unkind to the very birds, and nosediving
they leave their life beneath the towering cloud.
What's more, to move pasture is now no remedy:
the therapies attempted work ill. The experts give up,
Phillyra's son Chiron and Amythaon's son Melampus.   550
Loosed into light from Stygian gloom, ghastly Tisiphone
rampages, driving Plague and Fear before her,
and day on day upstirring rears her greedy visage higher.
The streams and their thirsting banks and sloped hills
    repeat
the bleating of flocks and their constant bellowing.
Now she deals out slaughter in droves, and heaps up

in stabulis turpi dilapsa cadavera tabo,
donec humo tegere ac foveis abscondere discunt.
nam neque erat coriis usus, nec viscera quisquam
560   aut undis abolere potest aut vincere flamma.
ne tondere quidem morbo inluvieque peresa
vellera nec telas possunt attingere putris;
verum etiam invisos si quis temptarat amictus,
ardentes papulae atque immundus olentia sudor
membra sequebatur, nec longo deinde moranti
tempore contactos artus sacer ignis edebat.

in their very stalls the corpses decomposing with foul rot,
until men learn to seal them up with dirt and bury them in
    pits.
For neither could the hides be used, nor could anyone
purge the vitals clean with water, nor contain it by bonfire. 560
They could not even shear the fleeces, eaten through with
    fester
and filth, nor touch the tainted yarn:
for if anyone should but try on the malignant robes,
fevered boils and vile sweat would run over
his reeking limbs: he would have no long hour to wait
for the accursed fire to devour his infected flesh.

Book Four

LIBER IV

Protinus aërii mellis caelestia dona
exsequar. hanc etiam, Maecenas, aspice partem.
admiranda tibi levium spectacula rerum
magnanimosque duces totiusque ordine gentis
mores et studia et populos et proelia dicam.
in tenui labor; at tenuis non gloria, si quem
numina laeva sinunt auditque vocatus Apollo.

Principio sedes apibus statioque petenda,
quo neque sit ventis aditus (nam pabula venti
ferre domum prohibent) neque oves haedique petulci
floribus insultent, aut errans bucula campo
decutiat rorem et surgentis atterat herbas.
absint et picti squalentia terga lacerti
pinguibus a stabulis, meropesque aliaeque volucres
et manibus Procne pectus signata cruentis;
omnia nam late vastant ipsasque volantis
ore ferunt dulcem nidis immitibus escam.
at liquidi fontes et stagna virentia musco
adsint et tenuis fugiens per gramina rivus,
palmaque vestibulum aut ingens oleaster inumbret,
ut, cum prima novi ducent examina reges
vere suo ludetque favis emissa iuventus,
vicina invitet decedere ripa calori,
obviaque hospitiis teneat frondentibus arbos.

BOOK FOUR

Onward. The celestial gifts of honey from the sky
I will sound. Attend this part as well, O Maecenas.
The wondrous spectacle of a tiny world –
bold-hearted princes, a whole nation's customs
and passions and citizens and wars will I describe for you.
In miniature my labour, but no miniature glory, if adverse
divinities allow it, if Apollo hears my prayer.

First, a settled site for your bees must be sought,
where no winds may access (for winds prevent them
bringing home their food), nor sheep or tussling kids   10
romp upon the flowers, nor rambling heifer in the
    meadows
to shake off the dew and erode the plantlife.
Keep gaudy lizards with their scaly backs
from the rich cells, and the bee-eater and other birds,
and Procne, breast stained with bloody hands.
For these devastate completely, far and wide, snatching
in their mouths bees on the wing, sweet snacks for their
    rough nestlings.
But let pure springs and pools greening with moss
be near, and a trickling stream slipping through the grass,
and let a palm or spreading oleaster overshade the
    vestibule,   20
so that when new kings lead out the first swarms
in dear spring and the youth frolic free of the honeycomb,
a nearby bank may woo them to dodge the heat
and a wayside tree may charm with its leafy welcome.

in medium, seu stabit iners seu profluet umor,
transversas salices et grandia conice saxa,
pontibus ut crebris possint consistere et alas
pandere ad aestivum solem, si forte morantis
sparserit aut praeceps Neptuno immerserit Eurus.
30 haec circum casiae virides et olentia late
serpylla et graviter spirantis copia thymbrae
floreat, inriguumque bibant violaria fontem.
ipsa autem, seu corticibus tibi suta cavatis
seu lento fuerint alvaria vimine texta,
angustos habeant aditus: nam frigore mella
cogit hiems, eademque calor liquefacta remittit.
utraque vis apibus pariter metuenda; neque illae
nequiquam in tectis certatim tenuia cera
spiramenta linunt, fucoque et floribus oras
40 explent, collectumque haec ipsa ad munera gluten
et visco et Phrygiae servant pice lentius Idae.
saepe etiam effossis, si vera est fama, latebris
sub terra fovere larem, penitusque repertae
pumicibusque cavis exesaeque arboris antro.
tu tamen et levi rimosa cubilia limo
ungue fovens circum, et raras superinice frondes.
neu propius tectis taxum sine, neve rubentis
ure foco cancros, altae neu crede paludi,
aut ubi odor caeni gravis aut ubi concava pulsu
50 saxa sonant vocisque offensa resultat imago.

Quod superest, ubi pulsam hiemem sol aureus egit
sub terras caelumque aestiva luce reclusit,
illae continuo saltus silvasque peragrant
purpureosque metunt flores et flumina libant
summa leves. hinc nescio qua dulcedine laetae
progeniem nidosque fovent, hinc arte recentis
excudunt ceras et mella tenacia fingunt.

In mid-water, whether it tranquil pools or flows along,
pile willows and enormous rocks across
that upon bridges aplenty they may rest and open
wings to the summer sun, if perforce the eastwind
has sprinkled upon the slowpokes, or dunked them
    headfirst into the deep.
Hereabout let flourish green cassia and far-fragrant   30
thyme and a garland of savory with its heady exhalations,
and let violet beds drink from the gurgling spring.
As for the hives: whether you have one stitched
from hollow bark or woven of limber wicker
let it have narrow entrances, for winter with its chill
congeals honey, and heat streams it away runny.
Either offence against the bees must be feared the same:
not for nothing do they striving smear with wax
fine cracks in their rooms, and with flower-paste fill up
seams, and store up glue collected for this very purpose,   40
stickier than birdlime or the pitch of Phrygian Ida.
Often, if rumour's true, in dug-out burrows
underground they snug their home, or deep within
    pumice-pores
are found, or in the cavity of a rotting tree.
Either way, do slick with smooth mud their crazed
    chambers,
cosying them up, and toss a few leaves on top.
Neither allow a yew too near the hive, nor fire
the redding crab at your hearth, nor trust a sunken bog
or where the stench of swamp is strong, or where hollow
the struck rocks ring and the voice's echo ricochets back.   50

When in rout the golden sun has driven winter
beneath the earth and unveiled with summer light the sky,
O then they wing the glades and forests,
harvest purple blooms and lightly sip
the river's surface. For this, cheered with an unfamiliar
    glee,
they nestle nests and larvae, for this they skilful mould
fresh wax and fashion sticky honey.

hinc ubi iam emissum caveis ad sidera caeli
nare per aestatem liquidam suspexeris agmen
60   obscuramque trahi vento mirabere nubem,
contemplator: aquas dulcis et frondea semper
tecta petunt. huc tu iussos adsperge sapores,
trita melisphylla et cerinthae ignobile gramen,
tinnitusque cie et Matris quate cymbala circum.
ipsae consident medicatis sedibus, ipsae
intima more suo sese in cunabula condent.

Sin autem ad pugnam exierint – nam saepe duobus
regibus incessit magno discordia motu,
continuoque animos volgi et trepidantia bello
70   corda licet longe praesciscere; namque morantis
Martius ille aeris rauci canor increpat et vox
auditur fractos sonitus imitata tubarum;
tum trepidae inter se coeunt pinnisque coruscant
spiculaque exacuunt rostris aptantque lacertos
et circa regem atque ipsa ad praetoria densae
miscentur magnisque vocant clamoribus hostem.
ergo ubi ver nactae sudum camposque patentis,
erumpunt portis: concurritur, aethere in alto
fit sonitus, magnum mixtae glomerantur in orbem
80   praecipitesque cadunt; non densior aëre grando,
nec de concussa tantum pluit ilice glandis.
ipsi per medias acies insignibus alis
ingentis animos angusto in pectore versant,
usque adeo obnixi non cedere, dum gravis aut hos
aut hos versa fuga victor dare terga subegit.
hi motus animorum atque haec certamina tanta
pulveris exigui iactu compressa quiescent.

*

Thus when you look up at their legion just unloosed
from the hive, up to the starred sky floating through liquid
    summer air,
and wonder at their cloud dark on the trailing wind,   60
take note: for sweet waters and sheltering leaves
they always beeline. Here scatter my prescribed delicacies:
rubbed balm, and tendrils of lowly waxflower,
and thrill up a tinkling sound, shaking Mother Cybele's
    cymbals all around.
On their own they'll settle upon the scented places, on their
    own
they'll burrow themselves by instinct in inmost chambers.

But if for battle they've burst forth – for often
between two kings strife with great riot swoops:
at once the rancour of the throng, the hearts churning
for war you can sense from afar. For a martial reveille   70
of raucous brass rattles the laggards, and a buzz
is heard like the broken blast of bugles.
Then all hopped-up they muster themselves, flash wings,
whet stingers with jaws and cinch up muscles,
and round the king right up to his battle-post thronged
they swarm and with great ruckus call out the foe.
Thus when they find a rainless spring day and open field
they charge from their coverts: *Clash!* Noise through
highest air, massed and bunched into a great ball
then headlong they crash! Not thicker hail from vast
    heaven   80
nor acorns hail so from the shaken oak.
The princes themselves among the battle lines with striking
    wings:
great hearts thump inside their tiny breasts,
ever so steadfast not to surrender till severe the victor
drives this side or that to turn tail in flight.
These tremors of passion, these battles so dire
with a little dust tossed are quelled and come to rest.

*

Verum ubi ductores acie revocaveris ambo,
deterior qui visus, eum, ne prodigus obsit,
90 dede neci; melior vacua sine regnet in aula.
alter erit maculis auro squalentibus ardens.
nam duo sunt genera: hic melior, insignis et ore
et rutilis clarus squamis; ille horridus alter
desidia latamque trahens inglorius alvum.
ut binae regum facies, ita corpora plebis.
namque aliae turpes horrent, ceu pulvere ab alto
cum venit et sicco terram spuit ore viator
aridus; elucent aliae et fulgore coruscant
ardentes auro et paribus lita corpora guttis.
100 haec potior suboles, hinc caeli tempore certo
dulcia mella premes, nec tantum dulcia, quantum
et liquida et durum Bacchi domitura saporem.

At cum incerta volant caeloque examina ludunt
contemnuntque favos et frigida tecta relinquunt,
instabilis animos ludo prohibebis inani.
nec magnus prohibere labor: tu regibus alas
eripe; non illis quisquam cunctantibus altum
ire iter aut castris audebit vellere signa.
invitent croceis halantes floribus horti
110 et custos furum atque avium cum falce saligna
Hellespontiaci servet tutela Priapi.
ipse thymum pinosque ferens de montibus altis
tecta serat late circum, cui talia curae;
ipse labore manum duro terat, ipse feracis
figat humo plantas et amicos inriget imbris.

*

But when from the front you have recalled both
    commanders,
he who looks shabbier, lest he be a waste and a burden,
consign to extinction: let the better reign singly in his
    court.   90
He will glow with spots shagged in gold.
For two kinds there are: the nobler, distinguished in mien
and bright in burnished scales, the other unkempt
in his sloth, inglorious, dragging his fat paunch.
Just as the mould of kings is twofold, so too the
    commoners' bodies.
Some look rough and slovenly, as when out of thick dust
comes a wayfarer, parched, and spits dirt from his thirsty
mouth. Others gleam and fulgent flash
blazing in bodies trimmed with uniform flecks of gold:
this is the better breed, from these at the sky's appointed
    season   100
you will strain sweeter honey – so sweet, but more clear,
and fit to mellow the harsh taste of wine.

But when aimless flits the swarm, and gads about the sky,
and scorns the honeycombs, and leaves the hive to chill
you must curb their fickle spirits from these pointless
    antics.
It's no great task to curb them: you rip the kings' wings
    off –
while they cool their heels, no one will dare
take to the air or snatch up the banner from the
    encampment.
Let gardens breathing saffron flowers beckon,
and let the watchman against thieves and birds, guardian   110
Priapus of the Hellespont, protect with his willow-hook.
Let him whose care they are himself fetch thyme and pines
from mountain peaks, and plant them round about their
    lodge,
himself callous his hand with rugged work, himself plant
fruitful slips in the soil and water them with kind sprinklings.

*

Atque equidem, extremo ni iam sub fine laborum
vela traham et terris festinem advertere proram,
forsitan et, pinguis hortos quae cura colendi
ornaret, canerem, biferique rosaria Paesti,
120 quoque modo potis gauderent intiba rivis
et virides apio ripae, tortusque per herbam
cresceret in ventrem cucumis; nec sera comantem
narcissum aut flexi tacuissem vimen acanthi
pallentisque hederas et amantis litora myrtos.
namque sub Oebaliae memini me turribus arcis,
qua niger umectat flaventia culta Galaesus,
Corycium vidisse senem, cui pauca relicti
iugera ruris erant, nec fertilis illa iuvencis
nec pecori opportuna seges nec commoda Baccho.
130 hic rarum tamen in dumis olus albaque circum
lilia verbenasque premens vescumque papaver
regum aequabat opes animis, seraque revertens
nocte domum dapibus mensas onerabat inemptis.
primus vere rosam atque autumno carpere poma,
et cum tristis hiems etiamnum frigore saxa
rumperet et glacie cursus frenaret aquarum,
ille comam mollis iam tondebat hyacinthi
aestatem increpitans seram Zephyrosque morantis.
ergo apibus fetis idem atque examine multo
140 primus abundare et spumantia cogere pressis
mella favis; illi tiliae atque uberrima pinus,
quotque in flore novo pomis se fertilis arbos
induerat, totidem autumno matura tenebat.
ille etiam seras in versum distulit ulmos
eduramque pirum et spinos iam pruna ferentis
iamque ministrantem platanum potantibus umbras.
verum haec ipse equidem spatiis exclusus iniquis
praetereo atque aliis post me memoranda relinquo.

*

Indeed, were I not fast upon the very end of my labours
furling sails, and rushing to nose my prow shoreward,
perhaps how care in tillage bedizens the lush garden
I'd sing, and the rosebeds of twice-blooming Paestum,
how the chicory exults in the brook it drinks,   120
and the banks green in celery, and how twining through its
    vines
the cucumber swells into corpulence; nor should I keep
    silent
on late-blooming narcissus or the stalk of supple acanthus,
pale ivies and shore-loving myrtles.
For I remember how, beneath the towers of Tarentum's
    citadel
where dark Galaesus waters the golden fields,
I saw an old Corycian, who had a few acres
of godforsaken land – a patch not fertile for the plough-ox
nor fit for flocks nor favourable for the vine.
Yet here, planting well-spaced vegetables among the scrub, 130
white lilies and verbena, and the flimsy poppy,
in cheer he matched the wealth of kings, and late returning
home at night he loaded his table with banquets unbought.
First in spring to pluck roses, first in fall to pick apples,
and when lowering winter was still cracking rocks
with cold, and with ice bridling the coursing stream,
he was already cutting back the soft hyacinth's old growth,
chiding tardy summer and the westwind's delay.
Therefore this man was first to luxuriate in brood-bees
and an abundant swarm, first to collect foamy honey   140
from the squeezed comb, his lindens and pines most lush
and as many buds as his lavish tree bedecks itself
in early bloom, so many fruits it holds in ripe autumn.
What's more, mature the elms he set in widespread rows,
hard-barked the pear trees, blackthorns already bearing
    sloes,
the plane tree already providing shade for carouses.
But I prevented by my too-slight space
pass silent on and leave that tale for others after me.

*

Nunc age, naturas apibus quas Iuppiter ipse
150   addidit expediam, pro qua mercede canoros
Curetum sonitus crepitantiaque aera secutae
Dictaeo caeli regem pavere sub antro.
solae communis natos, consortia tecta
urbis habent, magnisque agitant sub legibus aevum,
et patriam solae et certos novere penatis,
venturaeque hiemis memores aestate laborem
experiuntur et in medium quaesita reponunt.
namque aliae victu invigilant et foedere pacto
exercentur agris; pars intra saepta domorum
160   narcissi lacrimam et lentum de cortice gluten
prima favis ponunt fundamina, deinde tenacis
suspendunt ceras; aliae spem gentis adultos
educunt fetus; aliae purissima mella
stipant et liquido distendunt nectare cellas;
sunt quibus ad portas cecidit custodia sorti,
inque vicem speculantur aquas et nubila caeli,
aut onera accipiunt venientum, aut agmine facto
ignavum fucos pecus a praesepibus arcent.
fervet opus, redolentque thymo fragrantia mella.
170   ac veluti lentis Cyclopes fulmina massis
cum properant, alii taurinis follibus auras
accipiunt redduntque, alii stridentia tingunt
aera lacu; gemit impositis incudibus Aetna;
illi inter sese magna vi bracchia tollunt
in numerum, versantque tenaci forcipe ferrum:
non aliter, si parva licet componere magnis,
Cecropias innatus apes amor urget habendi
munere quamque suo. grandaevis oppida curae

Now come: I will unfold what nature
Jupiter himself bestowed on bees, for which reward   150
following the ringing chants and clashing bronzes of the
    Curetes
they had fed the king of heaven deep within a Dictaean
    cave.
They alone in common rear their young, in partnership
    they hold
their city's habitations, and live out their lives under
    sovereign laws,
they alone recognize a fatherland and constant home,
and mindful of the coming winter endure summer toil
and in common store lay in their gleanings.
For some have charge of provisions, and by settled
    compact
busy in the fields; some within their houses' walls
lay down tears of the narcissus and sticky sap   160
from tree-bark as the first foundation of the hive, then
    drape up
viscous wax. Others train out the nation's hope,
the full-grown hatch; others pack in purest
honey, swelling the cells with liquid nectar.
There are those to whom guard duty at the gates falls by
    lot;
in turn they eye heaven's showers and overcast,
or receive loads from incomers, or in mustered squads
blockade the drones (that shiftless ruck) from the stalls.
The industry glows, and the fragrant honey breathes of
    thyme.
As when the Cyclopes from malleable ore   170
work lightning bolts, some with ox-hide bellows
suck and blow the air, others dunk the screaming bronze
in a cistern; Aetna groans beneath its anvilled charge;
they heave their arms with mighty force in alternating
rhythm, and turn the metal with pincing tongs:
just so, if one may small compare with great,
an innate love of gain pricks on Athenian bees
each in his own capacity. The elders warden the towns,

et munire favos et daedala fingere tecta.
180   at fessae multa referunt se nocte minores,
crura thymo plenae; pascuntur et arbuta passim
et glaucas salices casiamque crocumque rubentem
et pinguem tiliam et ferrugineos hyacinthos.
omnibus una quies operum, labor omnibus unus:
mane ruunt portis; nusquam mora; rursus easdem
Vesper ubi e pastu tandem decedere campis
admonuit, tum tecta petunt, tum corpora curant;
fit sonitus, mussantque oras et limina circum.
post, ubi iam thalamis se composuere, siletur
190   in noctem, fessosque sopor suus occupat artus.
nec vero a stabulis pluvia impendente recedunt
longius, aut credunt caelo adventantibus Euris,
sed circum tutae sub moenibus urbis aquantur
excursusque brevis temptant, et saepe lapillos,
ut cumbae instabiles fluctu iactante saburram,
tollunt, his sese per inania nubila librant.

Illum adeo placuisse apibus mirabere morem,
quod neque concubitu indulgent, nec corpora segnes
in Venerem solvunt aut fetus nixibus edunt;
200   verum ipsae e foliis natos, e suavibus herbis
ore legunt, ipsae regem parvosque Quirites
sufficiunt, aulasque et cerea regna refingunt.
saepe etiam duris errando in cotibus alas

fortify the hives and fashion daedal chambers.
Worn out, the young ones drag themselves home far into
    night,   180
legs thick with thyme. They feast on arbutes all around,
on grey-green willows, on cassia and red-flecked crocus,
on the sappy linden and dusky hyacinths.
Together their rest from labour, together their labour:
at dawn they rush out their gates, no dilly-dally; and when
    at last
the evening star exhorts them quit their forage
afield, then they head for their hutches, then restore their
    bodies.
A buzzing: they murmur around the doors and on the
    doorsteps.
Later, when they've tucked themselves into their chambers,
    hushed
is the night, well-earned sleep overtakes their tuckered
    limbs.   190
But truly, rain threatening, they don't venture far from
    their stalls
nor trust the sky when the eastwind advances,
but on all sides, safe beneath the city's ramparts, siphon up
    water
and attempt short sorties, and often take up pebbles, with
    which,
as a skiff unsteady on the tossing wave takes on ballast,
they balance themselves through the flimsy cloud.

You will marvel *this* custom has found favour among bees:
they indulge not in lovemaking, nor slacken their sinews
sluggish in venery, nor birth young in travail,
but alone the females gather up their children in their
    mouths   200
from leaves and herbs delectable, unmated they provide a
    king
and tiny citizens, and remodel their courts and waxy
    realms.
Often too, wandering among jagged flint they scrape

attrivere, ultroque animam sub fasce dedere:
tantus amor florum et generandi gloria mellis.
ergo ipsas quamvis angusti terminus aevi
excipiat (neque enim plus septima ducitur aestas),
at genus immortale manet, multosque per annos
stat fortuna domus, et avi numerantur avorum.

210   Praeterea regem non sic Aegyptus et ingens
Lydia nec populi Parthorum aut Medus Hydaspes
observant. rege incolumi mens omnibus una est;
amisso rupere fidem, constructaque mella
diripuere ipsae et cratis solvere favorum.
ille operum custos, illum admirantur et omnes
circumstant fremitu denso stipantque frequentes,
et saepe attollunt umeris et corpora bello
obiectant pulchramque petunt per vulnera mortem.

His quidam signis atque haec exempla secuti
220   esse apibus partem divinae mentis et haustus
aetherios dixere; deum namque ire per omnia
terrasque tractusque maris caelumque profundum;
hinc pecudes, armenta, viros, genus omne ferarum,
quemque sibi tenuis nascentem arcessere vitas;
scilicet huc reddi deinde ac resoluta referri
omnia, nec morti esse locum, sed viva volare
sideris in numerum atque alto succedere caelo.

Si quando sedem angustam servataque mella
thesauris relines, prius haustu sparsus aquarum
230   ora fove, fumosque manu praetende sequacis.

their wings, and freely give their lives under their load:
so great their love of flowers and the glory of honey-
    making.
Thus although the limit of a slender age awaits each one
(for never more than seven summers it's unskeined)
yet the race endures immortal, through unnumbered years
    stands fast
the fortune of the house, and their pedigree records
    ancestors of ancestors.

What's more, not Egypt nor great Lydia, nor the Parthian
    peoples,   210
nor the Hydaspean Medes so venerate their king.
Their king unharmed, the swarm has a single mind;
if lost, they break faith, tear down their stockpiled honey
and themselves dismantle the trellises of the hive.
He is protector of their works, him they revere and all
surround him with crowded noise and pack him in
    thronging,
and often lift him to their shoulders, and throw their bodies
into battle seeking among the wounds a beautiful death.

Following such signs and such habits, some
have said that bees enjoy a share of the divine mind   220
and ethereal draughts. For God moves through all things –
lands and the sea's expanse and deepest heaven.
Flocks, herds, men, all breeds of beasts . . .
from Him each at birth draws its fine-spun life,
it seems, and to Him all return at last: all things undone
restored, no place for death, but alive they fly
into the station of a star and mount to heaven's zenith.

If ever you want to breach the bees' tight courts, and
    uncache
hoarded honey from their treasuries, first with a handful of
    water
spritz and freshen your mouth, and hold out penetrating
    smoke.   230

illis ira modum supra est, laesaeque venenum
morsibus inspirant, et spicula caeca relinquunt
adfixae venis, animasque in vulnere ponunt.
bis gravidos cogunt fetus, duo tempora messis,
Taygete simul os terris ostendit honestum
Plias et Oceani spretos pede reppulit amnis,
aut eadem sidus fugiens ubi Piscis aquosi
tristior hibernas caelo descendit in undas.
sin duram metues hiemem parcesque futuro
240   contususosque animos et res miserabere fractas,
at suffire thymo cerasque recidere inanis
quis dubitet? nam saepe favos ignotus adedit
stellio et lucifugis congesta cubilia blattis
immunisque sedens aliena ad pabula fucus;
aut asper crabro imparibus se immiscuit armis,
aut dirum tiniae genus, aut invisa Minervae
laxos in foribus suspendit aranea cassis.
quo magis exhaustae fuerint, hoc acrius omnes
incumbent generis lapsi sarcire ruinas
250   complebuntque foros et floribus horrea texent.

Si vero, quoniam casus apibus quoque nostros
vita tulit, tristi languebunt corpora morbo –
quod iam non dubiis poteris cognoscere signis:
continuo est aegris alius color; horrida vultum
deformat macies; tum corpora luce carentum
exportant tectis et tristia funera ducunt;
aut illae pedibus conexae ad limina pendent,
aut intus clausis cunctantur in aedibus omnes
ignavaeque fame et contracto frigore pigrae.
260   tum sonus auditur gravior, tractimque susurrant,
frigidus ut quondam silvis immurmurat Auster,

Their rage surpasses measure: hurt, they breathe venom
into their stings, leave their stingers unseen
stuck in the vein, and lay down their lives in the wound.
Twice men gather the lavish yield, two seasons the harvest:
soon as Pleiad Taygete has shown her heavenly face
to earth and with her foot scorns the spurned flood of
    Ocean,
and when that same star fleeing rainy Pisces
more sadly sinks down from the sky into the wintry waves.
But if you fear a harsh winter, and would spare their future
and pity their crushed spirits and shattered fortunes, –   240
yet who to fumigate with thyme and prune off disused cells
would hesitate? For often unnoticed the newt has nibbled
the honeycombs, or whole dens of light-fleeing
    cockroaches,
or the no-account drone bellies up to another's ration,
or the vicious hornet has engaged their unequal arms
or the malevolent race of moths, or the spider spited by
    Minerva
has hung in the aisles her loose webs.
The more they're plundered, the more doggedly they'll
    press
to repair the wrack of their fallen race:
they'll cram the galleries and weave their garners about
    with nectar.   250

But if (since life has brought to bees our calamities too)
their bodies droop under grim disease –
which instantly you can discern by no vague signs:
sick, their colour changes at once, ragged leanness
disfigures their looks, then the bodies of those deprived of
    life
they bear out from their homes and lead the funeral march,
or linked by their feet they hang from the doorways,
or shut within chambers they linger, all
listless with starvation and numb with pinching cold.
Then a sound is heard, lower, a drawn-out mutter,   260
as sometimes cold the southwind hushes through the trees,

ut mare sollicitum stridit refluentibus undis,
aestuat ut clausis rapidus fornacibus ignis.
hic iam galbaneos suadebo incendere odores
mellaque harundineis inferre canalibus, ultro
hortantem et fessas ad pabula nota vocantem.
proderit et tunsum gallae admiscere saporem
arentisque rosas, aut igni pinguia multo
defruta vel psithia passos de vite racemos,
270   Cecropiumque thymum et grave olentia centaurea.
est etiam flos in pratis, cui nomen amello
fecere agricolae, facilis quaerentibus herba;
namque uno ingentem tollit de caespite silvam,
aureus ipse, sed in foliis, quae plurima circum
funduntur, violae sublucet purpura nigrae;
saepe deum nexis ornatae torquibus arae;
asper in ore sapor; tonsis in vallibus illum
pastores et curva legunt prope flumina Mellae.
huius odorato radices incoque Baccho
280   pabulaque in foribus plenis appone canistris.

Sed si quem proles subito defecerit omnis,
nec genus unde novae stirpis revocetur habebit,
tempus et Arcadii memoranda inventa magistri
pandere, quoque modo caesis iam saepe iuvencis
insincerus apes tulerit cruor. altius omnem
expediam prima repetens ab origine famam.
nam qua Pellaei gens fortunata Canopi
accolit effuso stagnantem flumine Nilum
et circum pictis vehitur sua rura phaselis,
290   quaque pharetratae vicinia Persidis urget,
et diversa ruens septem discurrit in ora
usque coloratis amnis devexus ab Indis
et viridem Aegyptum nigra fecundat harena,
omnis in hac certam regio iacit arte salutem.
exiguus primum atque ipsos contractus in usus
eligitur locus: hunc angustique imbrice tecti

as the sea hisses roiling in its outflowing swell,
as seethes in shut furnaces the furious blaze.
Now I suggest you burn fragrant galbanum
and run in honey through straws of reed
heartening them, calling the weary to familiar food.
It will help, too, to mix the flavour of pounded gall-nuts
with dried roses, or must made concentrate
over a good fire, or raisin-wine from the Psithian vine,
and Athenian thyme with heady-smelling centaury.   270
There also is a flower in the meadows, to which the name
  amellus
farmers gave, an easy plant to ferret out,
for from one clump it lifts a massy spray –
itself golden, but in its petals which splay thickly around
crimson sheens beneath dark violet;
often the gods' altars are garlanded with its woven
  wreaths,
bitter on the tongue its taste, in grazed vales
shepherds gather it, and near the winding waters of Mella.
Boil its roots in fragrant wine
and set it at their doors for food in heaping baskets.   280

But if a man's whole hive suddenly has failed
and he knows not whence to revive the breed in a new line,
time to unfold the famed discovery of the Arcadian master
and by what means the spoiled blood from slain bullocks
has often engendered bees. I'll unspool
the whole account, retracing from its earliest source.
For where the blessed race of Pellaean Canopus
dwell near the Nile pooling in its sprawling stream
and ride their acres in painted skiffs,
where quivered Persia's territory hedges, and the river   290
onrushing, spilled unbroken down from the swart Indians,
branches into seven separate mouths
and with its black silt fertilizes Egypt green,
the whole region rests its sure well-being on this art.
First a spot – narrow and secluded for this very purpose –
is chosen: this with a narrow tile roof

parietibusque premunt artis, et quattuor addunt,
quattuor a ventis obliqua luce fenestras.
tum vitulus bima curvans iam cornua fronte
300   quaeritur; huic geminae nares et spiritus oris
multa reluctanti obstruitur, plagisque perempto
tunsa per integram solvuntur viscera pellem.
sic positum in clauso linquunt, et ramea costis
subiciunt fragmenta, thymum casiasque recentis.
hoc geritur Zephyris primum impellentibus undas,
ante novis rubeant quam prata coloribus, ante
garrula quam tignis nidum suspendat hirundo.
interea teneris tepefactus in ossibus umor
aestuat, et visenda modis animalia miris,
310   trunca pedum primo, mox et stridentia pinnis,
miscentur, tenuemque magis magis aëra carpunt,
donec ut aestivis effusus nubibus imber
erupere, aut ut nervo pulsante sagittae,
prima leves ineunt si quando proelia Parthi.

Quis deus hanc, Musae, quis nobis extudit artem?
unde nova ingressus hominum experientia cepit?
pastor Aristaeus fugiens Peneia Tempe,
amissis, ut fama, apibus morboque fameque,
tristis ad extremi sacrum caput astitit amnis,
320   multa querens, atque hac adfatus voce parentem:
'mater, Cyrene mater, quae gurgitis huius
ima tenes, quid me praeclara stirpe deorum
(si modo, quem perhibes, pater est Thymbraeus Apollo)
invisum fatis genuisti? aut quo tibi nostri

and cramped walls they enclose, and add four windows
with slant light to front the four winds.
Then a calf with horns just arched upon his two-year brow
is fetched, with both his nostrils and the breath of his
     mouth,   300
despite great struggling, stopped up. After he's beaten to
     death
his carcass is pulped up, pounded through the unbroken
     hide.
They leave him lying thus in his pen, and stuff beneath his
     flanks
broken twigs, thyme and fresh cassia.
This is accomplished when first the Zephyrs drive the
     waves,
before the meadows blush so in new colour, before
chattering the swallow hangs her nest among the rafters.
Meanwhile, fluid warmed in the softening bones
stews, and creatures with ways wondrous to behold,
devoid of foot at first but soon buzzing at the wing,   310
brew up, and more and more take to the narrow air
until, like a shower poured from summer clouds
they burst forth, or like arrows from the plucked string
when light-armed Parthians engage the opening volley.

What god, O Muses, forged for us this art?
Whence did man's strange practice take its start?
The shepherd Aristaeus, flying Tempe on the Peneus
when his bees were lost (the story goes) to sickness and
     starvation,
lamenting stopped by the sacred spring at the stream's
     headwaters
much complaining, and prayed aloud his mother thus: 320
'Mother, O mother Cyrene, who commands these waters'
     depths,
why me? – why from the glorious line of gods
(if truly, as you claim, my father is Thymbraean Apollo)
did you bear me, hated by the Fates? Or where is your love
     of me

pulsus amor? quid me caelum sperare iubebas?
en etiam hunc ipsum vitae mortalis honorem,
quem mihi vix frugum et pecudum custodia sollers
omnia temptanti extuderat, te matre relinquo.
quin age et ipsa manu felicis erue silvas,
330   fer stabulis inimicum ignem atque interfice messis,
ure sata et validam in vitis molire bipennem,
tanta meae si te ceperunt taedia laudis.'

At mater sonitum thalamo sub fluminis alti
sensit. eam circum Milesia vellera Nymphae
carpebant hyali saturo fucata colore,
Drymoque Xanthoque Ligeaque Phyllodoceque,
caesariem effusae nitidam per candida colla,
[   ]
Cydippeque et flava Lycorias, altera virgo,
340   altera tum primos Lucinae experta labores,
Clioque et Beroe soror, Oceanitides ambae,
ambae auro, pictis incinctae pellibus ambae,
atque Ephyre atque Opis et Asia Deiopea
et tandem positis velox Arethusa sagittis.
inter quas curam Clymene narrabat inanem
Volcani Martisque dolos et dulcia furta,
aque Chao densos divum numerabat amores.
carmine quo captae dum fusis mollia pensa
devolvunt, iterum maternas impulit auris
350   luctus Aristaei, vitreisque sedilibus omnes
obstipuere; sed ante alias Arethusa sorores
prospiciens summa flavum caput extulit unda,
et procul: 'o gemitu non frustra exterrita tanto,
Cyrene soror, ipse tibi, tua maxima cura,
tristis Aristaeus Penei genitoris ad undam
stat lacrimans, et te crudelem nomine dicit.'

banished? Why did you enjoin me hope for heaven?
Look: even this very trophy of mortal life
which the skilful care of crops and herds had hardly
    hammered out
for me, for all my efforts, though you're my mother, I
    resign.
Nay – go and with your own hand uproot my fruitful
    orchards,
put hostile fire to my stables, destroy my harvest,   330
burn my crops and heft the stout axe against my vines,
if such spite for my glory has seized you!'

But his mother in her bedchamber beneath the river's
    depths
felt his clamour. Around her, nymphs spun Milesian fleeces
dyed with the deep colour of glass –
Drymo and Xantho and Ligea and Phyllodoce,
their hair poured shimmering upon their radiant necks,
Cydippe and golden Lycorias, one a maid,
the other having just suffered her first birth-pangs,   340
Clio and Beroe her sister, Ocean's daughters both,
both in gold, both in rainbowed hides arrayed,
and Ephyre and Opis and Asian Deiopea,
and last swift Arethusa with her arrows laid aside.
Among these Clymene gossiped of the frustrate vigilance
of Vulcan, of Mars' wiles and stolen pleasures,
and from Chaos on recounted the myriad loves of the gods.
While by this ballad captivated from the spindle they
    twisted
their soft work, again the grief of Aristaeus struck
his mother's ears, and upon their glassy chairs all   350
startled. But before the other sisters Arethusa
far surveying raised her golden head above the surface
    stream
and from afar: 'Your fright at so loud howling's not amiss,
O sister Cyrene! Himself, your dearest care,
Aristaeus heartsick by the waters of Father Peneus
stands weeping, and you he calls by name of *Cruelty*.'

huic percussa nova mentem formidine mater
'duc, age, duc ad nos; fas illi limina divum
tangere' ait. simul alta iubet discedere late
360   flumina, qua iuvenis gressus inferret. at illum
curvata in montis faciem circumstetit unda,
accepitque sinu vasto misitque sub amnem.
iamque domum mirans genetricis et umida regna
speluncisque lacus clausos lucosque sonantis
ibat, et ingenti motu stupefactus aquarum
omnia sub magna labentia flumina terra
spectabat diversa locis, Phasimque Lycumque
et caput, unde altus primum se erumpit Enipeus
unde pater Tiberinus et unde Aniena fluenta
370   saxosusque sonans Hypanis Mysusque Caicus,
et gemina auratus taurino cornua voltu
Eridanus, quo non alius per pinguia culta
in mare purpureum violentior effluit amnis.
postquam est in thalami pendentia pumice tecta
perventum et nati fletus cognovit inanis
Cyrene, manibus liquidos dant ordine fontis
germanae, tonsisque ferunt mantelia villis;
pars epulis onerant mensas et plena reponunt
pocula, Panchaeis adolescunt ignibus arae.
380   et mater 'cape Maeonii carchesia Bacchi:
Oceano libemus' ait. simul ipsa precatur
Oceanumque patrem rerum Nymphasque sorores,
centum quae silvas, centum quae flumina servant.
ter liquido ardentem perfundit nectare Vestam,
ter flamma ad summum tecti subiecta reluxit.
omine quo firmans animum sic incipit ipsa:

'Est in Carpathio Neptuni gurgite vates,
caeruleus Proteus, magnum qui piscibus aequor
et iuncto bipedum curru metitur equorum.

To whom his mother, struck to the quick with sudden
 dread, cries:
'Go! Lead him! Lead him to us! He may tread this porch
 divine.'
And so she commanded the deep river to yawn
apart, that the youth might enter on foot. Hunched up   360
into mountain-shape the waters stood around him,
and welcomed him into a vast chasm, inviting him beneath
 the current.
Now wondering at his mother's home, a watery realm,
at lakes closed in caves and echoing groves,
he went on, astonished by the mighty rush of waters –
every river gliding beneath the wide earth
he descried, distinct in their courses: Phasis and Lycus,
the spring from which deep Enipeus first jets forth,
from which Father Tiber, from which the Anian stream
and rocky raucous Hypanis, and Mysian Caicus,   370
and Eridanus, both horns on his bullish front gilt,
than which no other stream more violent flows
out over fertile farmland into the purple sea.
When he's come into her chamber, its ceiling hung with
 pumice,
and Cyrene understands her son's vain tears,
her sisters timely minister to his hands
with clear spring water, and bring close-shorn napkins.
Some lade the table with a banquet and set down brimming
cups. The altars burn with Panchaian flame.
His mother declared: 'Lift your goblets of Maeonian wine: 380
we offer to Ocean.' With that she prayed
to Ocean, father of all, and the sister nymphs
who a hundred woods, a hundred rivers guard.
Thrice with liquid nectar she sprinkled the blazing hearth,
thrice the flame flared up anew, shooting to the rooftop.
With this omen bolstering his spirits, she thus began:

'There is in Neptune's Carpathian depths a seer,
aquamarine Proteus, who paces out the wide ocean
on a chariot yoked with fish and hippocampi.

390   hic nunc Emathiae portus patriamque revisit
      Pallenen; hunc et Nymphae veneramur et ipse
      grandaevus Nereus; novit namque omnia vates,
      quae sint, quae fuerint, quae mox ventura trahantur;
      quippe ita Neptuno visum est, immania cuius
      armenta et turpis pascit sub gurgite phocas.
      hic tibi, nate, prius vinclis capiendus, ut omnem
      expediat morbi causam eventusque secundet.
      nam sine vi non ulla dabit praecepta, neque illum
      orando flectes; vim duram et vincula capto
400   tende; doli circum haec demum frangentur inanes.
      ipsa ego te, medios cum sol accenderit aestus,
      cum sitiunt herbae et pecori iam gratior umbra est,
      in secreta senis ducam, quo fessus ab undis
      se recipit, facile ut somno adgrediare iacentem.
      verum ubi correptum manibus vinclisque tenebis,
      tum variae eludent species atque ora ferarum.
      fiet enim subito sus horridus atraque tigris
      squamosusque draco et fulva cervice leaena,
      aut acrem flammae sonitum dabit atque ita vinclis
410   excidet, aut in aquas tenues dilapsus abibit.
      sed quanto ille magis formas se vertet in omnis,
      tam tu, nate, magis contende tenacia vincla,
      donec talis erit mutato corpore, qualem
      videris, incepto tegeret cum lumina somno.'

      Haec ait et liquidum ambrosiae defundit odorem,
      quo totum nati corpus perduxit; at illi
      dulcis compositis spiravit crinibus aura
      atque habilis membris venit vigor. est specus ingens
      exesi latere in montis, quo plurima vento

Just now the ports of Thessaly and his native Pallene   390
he revisits; him the nymphs venerate and ancient
Nereus himself, for the seer has seen all –
what is, what has been, what's spun out soon to come,
for such seemed good to Neptune, whose herds immense
of squalid seals he pastures beneath the swell.
Him, son, you first must clap in shackles, so that the whole
cause of malaise he may unriddle and rally your fortunes.
Without duress no counsel will he give, nor will you bend
        him
by imploring; turn stern force and chains upon your
        captive:
only against these his wiles will crash themselves to froth.   400
I myself, when the sun stokes up its midday heat,
when plants thirst and shade is more delightful to the flock,
will guide you to the old man's retreat, where weary from
        the waves
he withdraws, that you may come at him sprawled in easy
        sleep.
But when you hold him fast gripped in hands and shackles
then his multiform shapes will bamboozle you, and his
        wild-beast looks.
For suddenly he'll be a bristled boar, a deadly tigress,
a scaly dragon, a tawny-necked lioness,
or blast out the piercing hiss of flame and thus slip out
from his bonds, or melt into mere water and spill away.   410
But the more he turns himself into all shapes
the more, O son, hold firm his chains
until after his body's changing he is such
as you saw him when he lidded his eyes at the start of
        sleep.'

She spoke, and radiated ambrosia's pure perfume,
in which her son's whole body she enwrapped;
from his sleeked locks a sweet scent breathed,
and vigour came upon his nimble limbs. There is a spacious
        cavern
worn in a mountain's side, where by the wind many a wave

420 cogitur inque sinus scindit sese unda reductos,
     deprensis olim statio tutissima nautis;
     intus se vasti Proteus tegit obice saxi.
     hic iuvenem in latebris aversum a lumine Nympha
     collocat; ipsa procul nebulis obscura resistit.
     iam rapidus torrens sitientes Sirius Indos
     ardebat caelo, et medium sol igneus orbem
     hauserat; arebant herbae et cava flumina siccis
     faucibus ad limum radii tepefacta coquebant,
     cum Proteus consueta petens e fluctibus antra
430 ibat; eum vasti circum gens umida ponti
     exsultans rorem late dispergit amarum.
     sternunt se somno diversae in litore phocae;
     ipse, velut stabuli custos in montibus olim,
     Vesper ubi e pastu vitulos ad tecta reducit
     auditisque lupos acuunt balatibus agni,
     considit scopulo medius, numerumque recenset.
     cuius Aristaeo quoniam est oblata facultas,
     vix defessa senem passus componere membra
     cum clamore ruit magno, manicisque iacentem
440 occupat. ille suae contra non immemor artis
     omnia transformat sese in miracula rerum,
     ignemque horribilemque feram fluviumque liquentem.
     verum ubi nulla fugam reperit fallacia, victus
     in sese redit atque hominis tandem ore locutus
     'nam quis te, iuvenum confidentissime, nostras
     iussit adire domos? quidve hinc petis?' inquit. at ille:
     'scis, Proteu, scis ipse; neque est te fallere quicquam:
     sed tu desine velle. deum praecepta secuti
     venimus hinc lassis quaesitum oracula rebus.'

is driven and splits itself into secluded lagoons,   420
at times a safest anchorage for swamped mariners.
Inside, Proteus screens himself in the covert of a massive
      boulder.
Here the nymph stations the youth in ambush
away from the light; she herself waits far off, veiled in mist.
Soon the ravaging Dog Star which scorches the thirsty
      Indians
blazed in the firmament, and the fiery sun had devoured
      half
his wheel: the grasses parched, and sunken streams
baked in their dry throats, boiled down to slime by its rays,
when Proteus, seeking his usual cove came down
from the waves. Around him the race of the vast sea   430
revelled, sprayed briny droplets far and wide.
The seals stretched themselves out for sleep scattered along
      the shore.
He himself – just as at times the caretaker of cotes upon a
      hill
when the evening star leads home the calves from pasture
and with their bleating din the lambs whet the wolves –
sat on a rock in their midst and counted their number.
Now that Aristaeus gets his chance,
scarce he lets the old man settle his tired limbs
when with a mighty yell he rushes him, and claps him in
      shackles
where he lies. Proteus for his part not forgetful of his art   440
transforms himself into all wondrous things of the earth:
a flame, a horrible beast, a stream flowing.
But when no design wins deliverance, defeated
he returns to himself, and speaking at last with the mouth
      of a man
he asked, 'Now, sauciest youth, who charged you
to invade our home? What seek you here?' But Aristaeus:
'*You* know, Proteus – you above all know, nor can
      anything deceive you,
so *you* give up deceiving! Following the gods' behest
we come here, seeking an oracle for my flagging fortunes.'

450 tantum effatus. ad haec vates vi denique multa
ardentes oculos intorsit lumine glauco,
et graviter frendens sic fatis ora resolvit:

'Non te nullius exercent numinis irae;
magna luis commissa: tibi has miserabilis Orpheus
haudquaquam ob meritum poenas, ni fata resistant,
suscitat et rapta graviter pro coniuge saevit.
illa quidem, dum te fugeret per flumina praeceps,
immanem ante pedes hydrum moritura puella
servantem ripas alta non vidit in herba.
460 at chorus aequalis Dryadum clamore supremos
implerunt montis; flerunt Rhodopeiae arces
altaque Pangaea et Rhesi Mavortia tellus
atque Getae atque Hebrus et Actias Orithyia.
ipse cava solans aegrum testudine amorem
te, dulcis coniunx, te solo in litore secum,
te veniente die, te decedente canebat.
Taenarias etiam fauces, alta ostia Ditis,
et caligantem nigra formidine lucum
ingressus, Manisque adiit regemque tremendum
470 nesciaque humanis precibus mansuescere corda.
at cantu commotae Erebi de sedibus imis
umbrae ibant tenues simulacraque luce carentum,
quam multa in foliis avium se milia condunt,
Vesper ubi aut hibernus agit de montibus imber,
matres atque viri defunctaque corpora vita
magnanimum heroum, pueri innuptaeque puellae,
impositique rogis iuvenes ante ora parentum;
quos circum limus niger et deformis harundo

So he intoned. At this the seer finally under sturdy force   450
rolled his eyes blazing with grey-green light
and savagely gnashing teeth thus unsealed his mouth with
     the fates:

'The wrath of no mean deity hounds you.
You do penance for a sore offence. Heartbroken Orpheus
     stirs up
these punishments against you (did not Fate intervene) –
far less than your deserving! – and rages tormented for his
     wife reft away.
Just so: headlong along the river that she might escape you,
doomed girl, she didn't see the monstrous snake
before her feet hugging the banks in tall grass.
The chorus of her companion dryads with wailing rimmed   460
the mountain's peaks, the crags of Rhodope mourned,
and alpen Pangaea, the martial land of Rhesus and the
     Getae,
the Hebrus mourned, and Orithyia the northwind's Attic
     bride.
But *he*, consoling love's agony with his hollow-shell lyre,
sang you, sweet wife, you to himself on the lonely shore,
you with the rising day, you at the day's decline.
Even the jaws of Taenarus, the steep gates of Dis,
the grove shrouded in black dread
he entered, and approached the dead, and their terrible
     king,
and the hearts unversed in gentling to human prayers.   470
But by his monody shaken from the deepest pits of Erebus
came wispy shades, and ghosts of those deprived of light,
as many as the birds that by the thousand hide themselves
     in leaves
when evening's star or winter sleet drives them from the
     mountains . . .
mothers and men and, emptied of life, the bodies
of bold-hearted heroes, boys and unwed maidens
and youths lain on the pyres before their parents' stares.
Around them the black mire and grotesque cattails

Cocyti tardaque palus inamabilis unda
480   alligat et noviens Styx interfusa coercet.
quin ipsae stupuere domus atque intima Leti
Tartara caeruleosque implexae crinibus anguis
Eumenides, tenuitque inhians tria Cerberus ora,
atque Ixionii vento rota constitit orbis.
iamque pedem referens casus evaserat omnis,
redditaque Eurydice superas veniebat ad auras,
pone sequens (namque hanc dederat Proserpina legem),
cum subita incautum dementia cepit amantem,
ignoscenda quidem, scirent si ignoscere Manes:
490   restitit, Eurydicenque suam iam luce sub ipsa
immemor heu! victusque animi respexit. ibi omnis
effusus labor atque immitis rupta tyranni
foedera, terque fragor stagnis auditus Avernis.
illa 'quis et me,' inquit, 'miseram et te perdidit, Orpheu,
quis tantus furor? en iterum crudelia retro
fata vocant, conditque natantia lumina somnus.
iamque vale: feror ingenti circumdata nocte
invalidasque tibi tendens, heu! non tua, palmas.'
dixit et ex oculis subito, ceu fumus in auras
500   commixtus tenuis, fugit diversa, neque illum,
prensantem nequiquam umbras et multa volentem
dicere praeterea vidit; nec portitor Orci
amplius obiectam passus transire paludem.
quid faceret? quo se rapta bis coniuge ferret?
quo fletu Manis, quae numina voce moveret?
illa quidem Stygia nabat iam frigida cumba.
septem illum totos perhibent ex ordine mensis
rupe sub aëria deserti ad Strymonis undam

of Cocytus, revolting swamp that binds them with sluggish
    water
and Styx winding nine times around imprisons them.   480
Why, the very halls were astonished, and Death's inmost
Tartarus, and the Furies with livid snakes braided
in their hair, and Cerberus held agape his three mouths,
and the spin of Ixion's wheel halted with the wind.
And soon his steps retracing he had dodged every pitfall
and Eurydice restored was coming to the upper air
following behind (for that stipulation had Proserpina
    made)
when a sudden madness seized him, reckless loving –
truly forgivable, if Hell knew to forgive:
he stopped, and upon his own Eurydice, already at the very
    edge of light,   490
forgetful, alas! and his judgement overthrown . . . he
    looked back. Instantly
all his labour fell apart, broken the pitiless tyrant's pact,
and thrice thunder sounded over the pools of Avernus.
She cried, "O Orpheus, what has ruined wretched me and
    you,
what utter madness? Behold – again the cruel Fates
call me back, and darkness shrouds my swimming eyes!
And now, farewell – I am carried off cloaked in endless
    night,
stretching toward you helpless hands, O! yours no more!"
She cried, and sudden from his sight, like smoke mingling
into thin air, vanished away, and – as he clutched vainly   500
at shadows, longing to say so much . . . she never
saw him more, nor did the ferryman of Orcus
let him cross that swampy obstacle again.
What could he do? Where take himself, his wife twice
    snatched away?
With what sobs could he move Hades, with what word its
    powers?
Even now she was floating cold as death in the Stygian raft.
For seven whole months, month on month, they say,
beneath a skyscraping cliff by desolate Strymon's wave

flevisse, et gelidis haec evolvisse sub astris
510   mulcentem tigris et agentem carmine quercus;
       qualis populea maerens philomela sub umbra
       amissos queritur fetus, quos durus arator
       observans nido implumis detraxit; at illa
       flet noctem, ramoque sedens miserabile carmen
       integrat, et maestis late loca questibus implet.
       nulla Venus, non ulli animum flexere hymenaei.
       solus Hyperboreas glacies Tanaimque nivalem
       arvaque Rhipaeis numquam viduata pruinis
       lustrabat, raptam Eurydicen atque inrita Ditis
520   dona querens; spretae Ciconum quo munere matres
       inter sacra deum nocturnique orgia Bacchi
       discerptum latos iuvenem sparsere per agros.
       tum quoque marmorea caput a cervice revulsum
       gurgite cum medio portans Oeagrius Hebrus
       volveret, Eurydicen vox ipsa et frigida lingua,
       a miseram Eurydicen! anima fugiente vocabat:
       Eurydicen toto referebant flumine ripae.'

       Haec Proteus, et se iactu dedit aequor in altum,
       quaque dedit, spumantem undam sub vertice torsit.
530   at non Cyrene; namque ultro adfata timentem:
       'nate, licet tristes animo deponere curas.
       haec omnis morbi causa, hinc miserabile Nymphae,
       cum quibus illa choros lucis agitabat in altis,
       exitium misere apibus. tu munera supplex
       tende petens pacem, et facilis venerare Napaeas;
       namque dabunt veniam votis, irasque remittent.
       sed modus orandi qui sit prius ordine dicam:

he wept, and under the frozen stars spun out this song,
soothing tigers and enticing oaks with his dirge, 510
as mourning beneath the poplar shade the nightingale
laments her lost brood, which a rude ploughman
spying ripped unfledged from their nest, she sobs
nightlong, and on a branch perched her doleful song
renews, and fills full the sphere with dreary plaints.
No love, nor any wedding-song could bend his soul.
Lonely he would wander the Hyperborean ice, the snow-
crusted Tanais,
the steppes ever widowed by Rhipaean frosts,
wailing Eurydice wrested away and the gift of Dis
annulled – by which devotion spurned, the Thracian dames 520
amid their consecrated rites and midnight bacchant orgies
tore the youth apart and scattered him across the field's
expanse.
Even then, while down the middle of its rapids
the Hebrus, river of his father's realm, swept and rolled
his head ripped from its marble neck,
Eurydice his mere voice and cold tongue were calling,
O poor Eurydice as his spirit fled,
Eurydice the banks replied the whole river long.'

So said Proteus, and threw himself into the deep sea,
and where he dived the water whirled to foam beneath his
vortex.
But Cyrene stayed. Unsought she addressed him, shaken: 530
'Son, you may lay down your soul's heavy care.
Here the whole cause of sickness, for this the nymphs
with whose troupe she used to trip through ancient groves
woeful brought this woeful blight upon your bees.
Suppliant, you must extend
an offering, praying peace, and do homage to the lenient
wood nymphs,
for they will grant pardon for your orisons, and ease their
anger.
But first I will explain how you should supplicate in
sequence:

quattuor eximios praestanti corpore tauros,
qui tibi nunc viridis depascunt summa Lycaei,
540   delige et intacta totidem cervice iuvencas.
quattuor his aras alta ad delubra dearum
constitue, et sacrum iugulis demitte cruorem,
corporaque ipsa boum frondoso desere luco.
post, ubi nona suos Aurora ostenderit ortus,
inferias Orphei Lethaea papavera mittes
et nigram mactabis ovem, lucumque revises:
placatam Eurydicen vitula venerabere caesa.'
haud mora: continuo matris praecepta facessit:
ad delubra venit, monstratas excitat aras,
550   quattuor eximios praestanti corpore tauros
ducit et intacta totidem cervice iuvencas.
post, ubi nona suos Aurora induxerat ortus,
inferias Orphei mittit, lucumque revisit.
hic vero subitum ac dictu mirabile monstrum
aspiciunt, liquefacta boum per viscera toto
stridere apes utero et ruptis effervere costis,
immensasque trahi nubes, iamque arbore summa
confluere et lentis uvam demittere ramis.

Haec super arvorum cultu pecorumque canebam
560   et super arboribus, Caesar dum magnus ad altum
fulminat Euphraten bello victorque volentis
per populos dat iura viamque adfectat Olympo.
illo Vergilium me tempore dulcis alebat
Parthenope studiis florentem ignobilis oti,
carmina qui lusi pastorum audaxque iuventa,
Tityre, te patulae cecini sub tegmine fagi.

select four choice bulls, outstanding in form,
who now with your herd graze the green ridge of Lycaeus,
and as many heifers with necks unworked.   540
For these erect four altars at the goddesses' high shrines,
and from their throats cascade the hallowed blood,
and leave their oxen carcasses in a leafy grove.
Later, when the ninth dawn flaunts her rising,
you will send Lethean poppies to Orpheus as a funeral
     offering
and sacrifice a black ewe, and return to the grove.
There honour Eurydice, now appeased, with a slaughtered
     calf.'
No delay – like a shot he performs his mother's
     instructions:
to the shrines he comes, rears the altars assigned,
leads in four choice bulls, outstanding in form   550
and as many heifers with necks unworked.
Later, when the ninth dawn had paraded her rising,
he sends a funeral offering to Orpheus and returns to the
     grove.
Here – . . . They spot a wonder, sudden and marvellous
to tell: in the oxens' liquified guts and through the whole
belly, bees buzz and swarm through the split flanks
and trail in unending clouds, and now surge
to a treetop and dangle in clusters from the limber boughs.

This I sang, about the care of fields and flocks
and about trees, while Caesar the great thundered in war   560
beside the deep Euphrates, and conqueror dealt out
laws to ready nations and pursued his course to heaven.
I, Virgil, at that time by sweet Parthenope
nurtured, flourishing in the study of inglorious leisure,
I who toyed with shepherd songs, and bold with youth,
sang you, Tityrus, beneath a vault of spreading beech.

Notes

BOOK ONE

Virgil's first book addresses the cultivation and harvest of grain crops.

1–4   *What cheers . . . thrifty bees:* Virgil lays out in these lines the four
subjects of the *Georgics'* four books: grain and tillage, viticulture,
animal husbandry, and beekeeping.

2   *wed vines:* Vines are 'wedded', or joined, to larger trees for
support.

5–6   *brightest fires / of heaven:* The sun and the moon, also invoked
by Varro in *Res Rusticae* 1.1.5.

7   *Liber and generous Ceres:* The chief deities of Book Two's viticul-
ture and Book One's agriculture.

10   *Fauns:* Goat-legged men, associated with the subject of Book
Three: the care of herds.

14   *genius of the groves:* Aristaeus, son of Apollo and the nymph
Cyrene, who farmed on the island of Cea, and whose beekeeping
trials are recounted in the last half of Book Four – though his
mention here has nothing to do with bees.

16   *Tegean Pan:* Virgil calls upon the Greek god to leave his native
Arcadian haunts, including the mountains Lycaeus and Maen-
alus, and lend his help to Italy.

19   *swain who trained us in the curving plough:* Triptolemus, inven-
tor of agriculture and a prince of Eleusis, a region of Greece
associated with the religion of Demeter.

24   *Caesar:* Virgil here refers to Octavian, later known as Caesar
Augustus, adoptive son of the late Julius Caesar.

28   *bright mother's myrtles:* Venus, the mother of Aeneas, is thus the
legendary forebear of Octavian.

34   *Virgin and the claws that chase her:* Virgil uses the Greek names
for the constellations Virgo and Scorpio, *Erigone* and *Chelae*.

68   *as Arcturus rises:* In early September.

93   *the northwind*: Although Virgil inherits a long linguistic tradition
      that identifies directional winds by their deities (Zephyr as the
      god of winds from the west, Auster from the south, Boreas
      the god of winds from the north, and Eurus the east), such
      anthropomorphic figuring of the winds is an echo of signification
      rather than an active evocation of gods in Virgil's text. Neverthe-
      less, Virgil's language does communicate that winds from each
      direction are distinct entities. This translation has attempted to
      preserve a sense of each wind's discrete character by identifying
      each wind using a single word – here, northwind – as opposed to
      two words (e.g., north wind, which would flatten the directional
      designation into mere modifier) or capitalization (e.g., North-
      wind, which veers into apotheosis).

96   *does golden Ceres smile on him from high Olympus!:* That is,
      rewards him with a rich harvest.

104   *Why mention him:* That is, in light of the abundance provided by
      propitious weather. Of course, Virgil mentions these industrious
      fellows anyway, indicating that labour must compensate for less
      than paradisaical conditions.

121   *The Father himself:* Jupiter, whose reign is characterized by
      labour, in contrast to the idylls of the Saturnian 'Golden Age'.

131   *secreted fire:* When Prometheus tricked Zeus into choosing sacri-
      fices of bones and fat over meat, Zeus hid fire from humans in
      revenge. In response, Prometheus stole fire from Zeus and shared
      it with mortals.

163–5 *Ceres ... baccant sanctity:* The Latin here calls her *Eleusinae
      matris*, 'Eleusinian Mother'. Her Greek equivalent, Demeter, was
      revered by the region of Eleusis, near Athens. The Eleusinian
      king, Celeus, was father to Triptolemus (see note on 1.19).
      Iacchus (or Bacchus) was also prominent in the Eleusinian agri-
      cultural religion; the winnowing-fan was used in sacrificial cere-
      monies to signify that the souls of worshippers were, like
      winnowed grain, purged of impurities.

199   *So by decree:* i.e., by Jupiter; see note on 1.121.

204–205 *Arcturus, / the bright Snake, the days of the Kids:* The star
      Arcturus in the constellation Boötes appears in the eastern sky
      in springtime and sets in the autumn, as do the Kids, three small
      stars above the bright star Capella, thought by the Greeks to
      honour the she-goat who suckled the infant Zeus. Draco (the
      Snake), like its near neighbour the North Star, does not set,
      making it a fixture in navigation.

208 *Libra:* The Scales, here imagined balancing night and day at the autumnal equinox.

217 *the dazzling Bull with gilded horns opens the year:* Virgil refers to the beginning of the agricultural calendar, when the April sun enters the constellation Taurus, the Bull. Virgil's description evokes the gilded horns of the sacrificial bullocks at Roman festivals.

218 *the Dog Star:* Sirius, which sets in April, seems to be backing down from the great Bull.

221 *Pleiades:* Virgil calls this constellation *Eoae Atlantides*, 'Daughters of Atlas', one of whom is Maia (1.225). It sets on the morning of 11 November. Virgil counsels wheat farmers to wait until mid-November to sow.

222 *blazing Crown's sovereign star:* The constellation Corona is named for the crown of Ariadne of Cnossos, which was set in the sky by her lover, Bacchus.

231 *For this:* That is, to give men signs for planting.

233–8 *Five zones comprise the firmament ... of God are granted:* Virgil's description of the physical world begins by discussing zones of the sky, whose effects are felt in the corresponding terrestrial zones below. Between a sweltering equatorial zone and two icy polar regions lies a temperate climate, ideal for man and for his agricultural pursuits. Virgil's geography relies heavily on the *Hermes* of Eratosthenes, an Alexandrian scholar of the third century BC.

240–43 *As the earth ... infernal:* Here the already complex description becomes a bit baffling: Virgil seems to assign a 'downward' position both to the southern hemisphere and to the Underworld.

244–5 *Serpent ... Bears:* These northern constellations – Draco, Ursa Major and Ursa Minor – never set, and thus never plunge into the ocean.

247–51 *There, they say ... the late hour's lights:* Here again, Virgil appears to be making use of contrasting geographical theories, first considering an arrangement of the universe which situates an Underworld beneath our feet, but also incorporating features of a round-earth model.

252 *So:* That is, having familiarized ourselves with these zones and stars.

265 *willow-cords:* In the Latin, *Amerina ... retinacula*, 'ties from Ameria', a region evidently known for its willows.

280 *those brothers:* Otus and Ephialtes, sons of Queen Iphimedia and

Poseidon (or Neptune), whose attempt to overthrow the gods Homer relates in the *Odyssey* 11.305–320.

299 *strip to plough, strip to sow:* A quotation from Hesiod's *Works and Days*, line 381.

309 *Balearic sling:* Hunting device from the Balearic Islands, in the western Mediterranean Sea near modern Spain.

335 *Fearing this:* That is, the chaos of stormy nature, which threatens the work of cultivation.

351–460 *That by sure signs ... you'll see the forests reel:* Virgil models his meteorology on the *Phaenomena* of Aratus, specifically the earlier work's section on 'weather signs' (roughly lines 730–1150).

398–9 *The halcyons ... catch the warm sun:* Mythical birds thought to nest and brood on the sea during a stretch of fourteen calm days in winter. Here, the weather is so fine that the halcyons need not stay ashore to keep warm.

404 *the owl rehearses her bootless evensong:* Though the owl's hoot was supposed to call down rain, these mild days frustrate that omen.

405 *Nisus:* King of Megara, and father of Scylla. She fell in love with Minos as he besieged Megara, and for his sake cut off the enchanted purple lock of hair from her father's head, causing the city to fall to the enemy. She was turned into a mythical bird, the *ciris*, and he into an osprey, ever in pursuit of her.

418 *Jove, wet from the south:* In the Latin, *Iuppiter uvidus Austris*, idiomatic for a rainy sky.

419–20 *condenses what was late dispersed, disperses / what was dense:* Virgil seems to be describing changes in humidity and barometric phenomena.

466–8 *It's he who ... eternal night:* The historical record indicates that the year 44 BC, in which Caesar was assassinated, saw unusual atmospheric phenomena, including a solar eclipse in November of that year.

474 *Germany heard the crash of arms throughout the sky:* That is, because of Germany's proximity to Roman operations.

489–90 *Thus Philippi again saw Roman troops / clash sword with fellow sword among themselves:* The first such clash was between Julius Caesar and Pompey at the Battle of Pharsalus in 48 BC, in Thessaly. Though this first battle was far from the second battle at Philippi in Macedonia, Virgil renders their temporal proximity as a spatial one.

498–9 *Gods of my fathers, heroes of the land, Romulus / and mother*

Vesta: Virgil invokes the aid of ancestral deities: anciently worshipped Vesta and the Lares and Penates, household gods brought by Aeneas from Troy. The *Indigetes*, whose number includes Romulus, are deified national heroes, like Aeneas (see the *Aeneid* 12.794).

499–500 *Tuscan Tiber / and the regnant Roman hill:* The Tiber river springs from, and flows through, Etruria. The palatial and principal hill of Rome is the *Palatia* or Palatine.

501 *this noble stripling:* Octavian, later Caesar Augustus.

503 *Laomedon's perjury at Troy:* King of Troy, Laomedon bilked Apollo and Neptune out of their promised reward after they helped to build the walls of Troy. The long period of civil war was seen as divine punishment for Rome's inherited guilt.

503–5 *long the courts ... Caesar:* Virgil returns again to the subject of Octavian's anticipated immortality (see 1.24–25).

510 *Euphrates:* Here a figure for attacking Parthians.

BOOK TWO

In this book, Virgil takes as his subject the care of vine-crops.

2 *Bacchus:* Virgil's attention now turns to grapevines, olives and other trees.

4 *winepress sire:* One of Bacchus' Greek epithets, *Lenaios*, identifies him with the winepress.

9 *nature is versatile:* Indeed, the versatility Virgil describes can seem overwhelming, but it is governed by a certain logic. This section begins with a thirteen-line consideration of wild methods of propagation: spontaneous, from fallen seeds, and from the root of the tree. The next thirteen lines proceed to methods of cultivated propagation, including the planting of suckers, stakes, layers, cuttings from high in the tree, growing from a piece of trunk, and grafting and budding.

14–16 *Some spring ... by Greeks:* Virgil distinguishes between two kinds of oak here, the *aesculus* and the *quercus*; the first seems to be characterized by larger and more abundant leaves. For a lengthy discussion of oak varieties, see John Sargeaunt's *The Trees, Shrubs, and Plants of Virgil.*

15 *Jovan groves:* Refers to the oak groves of Dodona, location of Zeus' – Roman Jupiter's – oracle.

18 *Delphic laurel:* The Latin *Parnasia laurus* or 'laurel of Parnassus'

alludes to Apollo's Delphic oracle on the mountain of Parnassus.

38   *Ismarus ... Taburnus:* After imagining the Thracian mountain
     Ismarus covered in vines, Virgil then shifts location and situates
     the olives on an Italian mountain, Taburnus. This pairing of
     Greek and Roman sites mirrors the poem's recurrent appropri-
     ation of classical Greek *topoi* into contemporary Roman formu-
     lations. Virgil's Latin invokes Bacchus, god of the vine, to
     represent vines themselves.

64   *Cyprian myrtles:* The Latin *Paphiae ... myrtus* refers to Paphos,
     a town in Cyprus fabled to be the birthplace of Venus, to whom
     the myrtle was sacred.

66   *Hercules:* The hero adorned himself with a crown of leaves after
     bringing Cerberus, the three-headed dog who guards the gates
     of Hades, up from the Underworld.

87   *Alcinous' orchards:* Alcinous, King of the Phaeacians, entertained
     Odysseus in Homer's *Odyssey* (7.112–32). His wondrous gar-
     dens produced abundant fruit year-round.

88–9 *Syrian pears, Crustumian pears, pears that heavy / fill the hand:*
     In his *Natural History,* Pliny the Elder praises pears from Syria
     and Crustumerium, a city in Latium in the west of Italy. The
     Latin *piris gravibus volemis* describes a large pear, the *volema,*
     whose name seems to refer to the way it fills the *vola* or palm.

89–102 *On our grapetrees ... buxom clusters:* Virgil's catalogue of
     wines takes in a wide geographical area. *Methymna* is a town on
     the Aegean island of *Lesbos. Thasos,* too, is an Aegean island.
     Mareotis is a lake near Alexandria, in Egypt. The geographic
     provenance of the *Psithian* wines is not known, and the *Lagean,*
     likewise, is a mystery, though its etymological link with Greek
     λαγός or 'hare' has suggested to some readers that this variety
     of grape ripens speedily. The *Rhaetic* came from a region in the
     northern Roman Empire, over the Alps from Italy. The *Falernian*
     wine comes from Campania, south of Rome, where Virgil owned
     an estate, and *Aminnean vines* were a variety grown in Campania
     as well. *Tmolian* wines come from Mount Tmolus in Asia Minor,
     Phanean from the Aegean island of Chios. *Argitis,* a white wine
     named because of its shining whiteness (from the Greek ἀργός,
     meaning 'shining, bright'). The *Rhodian vine* comes from the
     island of Rhodes off the coast of Asia Minor. Finally, the *Bumast*
     derives its name from the Greek μαστός or 'breast'.

115 *Scyths:* Virgil uses the term *Geloni,* a Scythian tribe in what is
     now southern Russia.

121 *from leaves China combs its silky integuments:* Based on the

mistaken notion that silk grew on trees. Virgil uses the term *Seres*, which connotes the cultivation of silk ('sericulture'), to indicate the far-off Chinese.

122 *Abyss:* That is, at the ends of the earth, on the coast of great Ocean.

126 *Media:* Here grew the citron, which serves as an emetic, according to Virgil's source, Theophrastus' *Historia Plantarum* 4.4.2.

129 This translation omits the line which appears at this point in some early manuscripts. The line, *miscueruntque herbas et non innoxia verba*, also appears at 3.283, where it makes much more sense in context.

140 *no bulls:* Italy, Virgil claims, possesses no mythic features, such as the fire-breathing bulls tamed by Jason and yoked to sow the teeth of the Theban dragon at Colchis, whence sprang warriors.

143 *Massic nectar:* Wine grown on a Mount Massicus in Campania, Virgil's home in adulthood.

147 *Clitumnus:* The bulls raised near this Umbrian river were thought to have gained their snowy colour by drinking from its springs. The bulls were bred for triumphal sacrifices.

152 *monkshood:* This may be poetic licence on Virgil's part, since monkshood does actually grow in Italy, although Sargeaunt claims that Virgil refers here to a poisonous pale yellow monkshood, which resembled the harmless aconite.

158–9 *up north / and down south:* The *Mare superum* or Adriatic Sea, and the *Mare inferum* or Tyrrhenian Sea.

161–4 *Lucrine . . . froth:* The Portus Julius or Julian Port was constructed in 37 BC by Agrippa, chief Roman general of the mid-first century BC. The natural shoreline protecting Lake Lucrine from the Gulf of Naples was replaced with a rocky breakwater which was open to let ships through. Lake Lucrine was connected with Lake Avernus by means of a man-made channel, creating an inner and outer harbour.

167 *Marsians:* Virgil begins his survey of Italian peoples by region with these inhabitants of south-central Italy, regarded as fierce warriors.

169–70 *Deciuses and Mariuses and mighty Camilluses, / war-tempered Scipios:* Men the like of these famous Roman figures.

172 *the unwarlike Indian:* Virgil's *imbellum . . . Indum* seems to refer to Asiatic peoples generally.

173 *Saturnian land:* Though, of course, the idyllic state of the Saturnian (or Golden) Age stands in opposition to the agricultural labour that concerns the *Georgics*.

176 *the song of Ascra:* Here again, Virgil invokes the Greek tradition
only to appropriate it for Rome, referencing Hesiod of Ascra,
the influence of whose *Works and Days* is evident especially in
Books One and Two of the *Georgics.*

181 *Minerva's groves:* Virgil refers to the goddess by her Greek name,
Pallas Athena.

196 *crop-spoiling goats:* See 2.373–381 on the sacrifice of goats to
Bacchus as a revenge for the harm their bite does to plants.

198 *forlorn Mantua:* Virgil's native town, lamented in the *Eclogues*
thus: '*superet modo Mantua nobis, / Mantua vae miserae nimium
vicina Cremonae . . .*' ('Let Mantua be spared for us, / Woeful
Mantua, too near desolate Cremona . . .' [9.27–28]). Virgil's
countrymen had their land seized by Caesar Augustus so that
returning soldiers could be settled there after the Battle of Philippi
(42 BC).

207 *enraged the ploughman:* The ploughman is angry, it seems,
because the land has been so long neglected that it is overgrown,
which would otherwise be good arable land.

225–6 *the banks of the Clanius, / unsparing of desolate Acerrae:* The
River Clanius flooded periodically, leaving nearby floodplain
towns depopulated – including Acerrae.

229 *Bacchus:* Virgil refers to the wine-god here as *Lyaeus*, a Greek
epithet appropriately meaning 'deliverer from care'.

257 *toxic yew trees:* The leaves and seeds of this cold-loving tree are
harmful to animals – see 4.47. The yew, like the ivies of the next
line, do well in cold northerly climates and soils.

301 *they love the earth too much!:* So much so, Virgil suggests, that
cuttings from the lower parts of the tree, closest to the earth,
flourish best.

320 *the white stork:* Virgil doesn't name the bird, calling it rather
candida . . . avis or 'white bird', but the description 'foe to trailing
snakes' provides a clue to the bird's identity, since the stork preys
on snakes.

321–2 *the blazing sun / already blown past summer has not yet
nuzzled winter with his team:* The sun-god, a role assigned both
to Apollo and to Helios, drove a flame-bright chariot across the
sky over the course of a day. His course, naturally, veered north
during the summer months and south during the winter months.

325 *Heaven:* Virgil identifies Jove, the Father, with the sky over which
he reigns.

329 *the rut:* Virgil here refers to Venus, the goddess associated with
sexual activity.

334 *the gusting North:* Aquilo, the northwind.

340–41 *earthen line / of men:* In some manuscripts, this passage reads *virumque / ferrea progenies* or 'iron line of men' – replacing *terrea* or 'earthen' with *ferrea* or 'iron'. But Virgil's vision here of spring at the dawn of creation argues for an essential sympathy between man and earth – a sort of innate perceptive connection that ends with Jupiter's institution of toil (see 1.121–128) and the beginning of the age of iron tools.

381 *time-honoured tragedies:* The word 'tragedy' derives from the Greek word τράγος or 'goat' (in Latin, *caper*).

382 *Theseus' Athenian sons:* Virgil refers to the Athenians by mentioning the legendary Athenian king, Theseus. The Athenian *Thesidae* or 'sons of Theseus' developed tragedy, as well as wit-prizes, during Dionysian festivals.

384 *oiled goatskins:* Apparently a traditional festive contest involving balancing or cavorting on the greased and inflated skin of a sacrificial goat. The Greeks called this amusement ἀσκωλιάσμος, after the Dionysian festival at which it was performed.

385 *Ausonian farmers:* Ancient inhabitants of Campania. Although he conflates Ausonians with Trojans here, in the *Aeneid* Virgil explicitly distinguishes Ausonians from Trojans.

387 *concave bark:* Perfectly shaped for fashioning into masks.

392 *everywhere the god swivels his august countenance:* That is, the face of the little effigies of Bacchus, from 2.389.

406 *Saturn's hooked sickle:* Because Saturn castrated his father with a sickle or pruning-hook, he is often represented as bearing such a tool.

410 *Twice upon the vines floods the shade:* Two times each year, foliage must be pruned from vine-tops to allow sun to ripen the fruit.

412–13 *Praise a vast estate, / till a small one:* A familiar proverb, used previously by Hesiod and Cato, among others.

413–15 *gnarled broom-shoots ... willow-stand taxes us:* These plants were used as twine for tying up vines.

433 This translation omits the line which appears at this point in some early manuscripts, reading *et dubitant homines serere atque impendere curam?* which asks, in the face of Nature's generosity, 'can men scruple to sow and spend their labour?' However, the line's immediate context in this poem deals not with man's labour but rather with the lavish open-handedness of Nature, the fruits that require no labour, like the olive. The line in question is regarded by many editors as an interpolation.

455–7 *Bacchus has given us grounds . . . a giant flagon:* The legendary
battle between the Centaurs and the Lapiths – enraged by im-
moderate wine consumption at the wedding feast of Pirithous,
the Thessalian king – became a sort of cultural morality tale
against intoxication.

464 *Corinthian bronzes:* Virgil uses *Ephyreia*, an old name for
Corinth.

465 *Assyrian potions:* Virgil refers to the luxuriant purple dyes of
Tyre, which was anciently ruled for a time by Assyrian governors.

469 *Tempes:* Virgil invokes the idyllic Greek valley in order to
imagine all such sites of pastoral perfection.

474 *departing Justice:* Astraea, goddess of Justice, was the last immor-
tal to leave the earth at the end of its Saturnian peace. After her
departure, the Iron Age – and its attendant labour – ensued.

476 *whose mysteries I observe:* That is, in a priestly role.

484 *the chill blood circling my heart:* Sicilian philosopher Empedocles
(*c.* 490–430 BC) had located man's intellect in the blood sur-
rounding the heart.

497 *Dacians swooping in cahoots with Danube:* The Dacians lived
in what is now Romania. Virgil refers to the lower Danube by
its Roman name, *Hister*.

502 *the iron laws, the lunatic Forum, the office of public records:*
Laws, not theoretically necessary in the Golden Age of Saturn,
are thus associated with the fall into an Iron Age existence. The
populi tabularia or public archives were kept on the Capitoline
Hill, overlooking the Forum; Virgil's phrase evokes prosaic
bureaucracy.

506 *Tyrian purple:* Virgil's Latin *Sarrano* uses the old Latin name for
Tyre.

536 *Dictaean king:* Because Jupiter was believed to have been reared
on Mount Dicte in Crete.

537 *a godless race feasted on slaughtered steers:* Aratus and others
scorned the Bronze Age men who ate their figurative yoke-mates,
the oxen.

BOOK THREE

Book Three addresses animal husbandry, with special focus on herds
and flocks.

2 *O goatherd god of Amphrysus, and you Lycaean woods and rills:*

Apollo spent time as a shepherd on the shores of the Thessalian river Amphrysus. Pan is subtly evoked by Virgil's reference to the woods of Lycaea, in Arcadia, home to this god of flocks.

7   *Hippodamia and Pelops:* Pelops won Hippodamia to be his bride in a chariot race against her father's immortal horses, a contest he won by cheating. His *ivory shoulder* was fashioned by the gods; they reconstructed him after he'd been served to them in a stew by his enraged father Tantalus, but his shoulder had already been eaten by Ceres.

10   *if only life prolong:* Virgil speaks not of the completion of the *Georgics*, but of a future project (the *Aeneid*?). He describes the proposed poem as a temple to Caesar.

19   *Nemean groves:* Another Greek locale to conclude Virgil's catalogue of ancient stories and places, which he provides in order to argue his intent to seize the literary glories accorded to ancient Greece for Rome. The Nemean groves are the site of Hercules' triumph over the invulnerable lion, which feat initiated the Olympic Games. Virgil's phrase, *lucos ... Molorchi*, refers to the poor labourer Molorchus, in whose cottage Hercules rested before facing the lion.

20   *in rawhide gloves:* That is, boxing. This line imagines the traditional Greek Olympian games on the shores of the Italian Mincius.

24–5   *see the stage-scene ... the purple curtain:* The Latin *vel scaena ut versis discedat frontibus* seems to describe the rotation of three-faced side sets to display different scenes. The curtain was raised (not lowered) at the end of each scene. Here, the Britons woven on to the curtain seem themselves to be lifting it.

25–33   *embroidered Britons ... on two shores:* Beginning with the Britons, this section's wide geographical scope celebrates the power and reach of the Roman Empire.

31   *the Parthian so cocky in his dodging and back-flung arrows:* This people from south-east of the Caspian Sea waged a form of guerrilla warfare unfamiliar to the Romans.

32   *our two trophies snatched by force from foes to East and West:* Virgil is jumping the celebratory gun a bit. The battle-standards that Crassus (the governor of Syria and in league with Julius Caesar) had lost to the Parthians in 53 BC were not recovered until 20 BC, nearly nine years after the completion of the *Georgics*. Virgil must have been anticipating – or hoping – that Octavian would recapture them.

35–6   *the line of Assaracus ... architect of Troy:* These names look forward to the *Aeneid*. Tros, great-grandson of Zeus in the *Iliad*, sires Ilus (grandfather of Priam) and Assaracus (grandfather of Anchises). Mount Cynthus is on Delos, birthplace of Apollo, whom the line references as one of the builders of the Trojan walls.

37–9 *Contemptible Envy . . . insurmountable stone:* Those who envy the honours of Octavian and the achievement of Virgil face either the doom of Ixion's being bound to an ever-turning wheel by snakes or Sisyphus' insurmountable stone.

40 *Meanwhile:* Bringing us back to the *Georgics*, the task at hand.

46 *But soon:* Again anticipating an epic to come.

48 *Tithonus:* The mention of this brother of Priam provides yet another link between Caesar and ancient Trojan glory.

60 *The age for childbirth and formal wedlock:* Virgil's Latin invokes the goddess of childbirth, Lucina, and Hymen, god of marriage, references which anthropomorphize the cows.

89 *Spartan Pollux:* Virgil indicates Sparta by referencing one of its cities, Amyclae. The Spartans revered Pollux and his twin brother Castor as protectors of their military. According to legend, the twins founded Amyclae.

93 *swift Saturn:* Kronos (Saturn), the father of Jupiter, was caught by his wife Rhea *in flagrante delicto* with his mistress Phillyra. To escape, he turned himself into a horse, which caused the nymph to give birth to the Centaur Chiron.

97 *joyless task:* That is, sex.

115 *Pelethronic Lapiths:* For the relationship between Centaurs and Lapiths, see note on 2.455–7.

118 *Equal each task:* Training horses for racing or for battle.

127 *alluring toil:* Of stud-work.

146 *Silaran woods:* The groves surrounding the River Silarus.

148 *is asilus, called oestrus in the evolving Greek:* Virgil places the Roman name of the gadfly beside its Greek name, thus evoking a long line of literary references to this pest. Virgil's note that the Greek name 'changes' (in his term *vertere*) throughout Greek literature recognizes the evolution of language over time, and includes his own language in that process.

152–3 *With this monster . . . heifered Io:* After Jupiter seduced Io, a priestess of Juno, he turned her into a cow to keep the affair secret. When Juno found out she sent the gadfly to plague the unfortunate heifer.

204 *Belgian chariot:* Used in battle.

223 *the woods and sky:* To indicate the heavens, Virgil mentions Olympus, dwelling place of the gods.

258 *that young buck:* Though initially, in the context of all this animal frenzy, seeming to describe a stag, the reference is actually to Leander, who swam across the Hellespont by night to visit his beloved Hero. He was drowned in a storm, at news of which she killed herself.

264 *Bacchus' spotted lynxes:* These beasts were supposed to have drawn Bacchus' chariot.

267–8 *four Potnian / race-mares:* Glaucus, King of Corinth and son of Sisyphus, was killed by his chariot mares because he kept them away from stallions in order to conserve their strength. (Perhaps foolishly, he also fed them human flesh to make them fierce.) By denying them sex, he offended Venus.

283 *brewing up . . . spells:* See note on 2.129.

303–4 *when cold / Aquarius is setting:* That is, in February; *sprinkling* plays off the constellation's wet name, and *the year's horizon* refers to the Roman calendar year, which ends in February and begins anew in March.

306 *Milesian wools:* Fine wool may yield high profits, but Virgil urges us not to scorn the profits to be earned from milk.

311 *Cinyphian goat:* Bred along the shores of the River Cinyps.

313 *careworn mariners:* Sailors who wear hair-cloth jackets.

340 *their stockyards squatted with sparse gourbi-huts:* Virgil's Latin reads *raris habitata mapalia tectis. Mapalia* means something like sheep-camps, simple and mobile, and the word seems in its specificity to Libya to carry the same ethnographic sense as the modern 'villa' or 'barrio' – that is to say, a place name with a precise ethnic connotation, the word perhaps originating in the local tongue. This translation employs an updated version of that effect, using a term from modern Libya to communicate the foreignness of the habitation.

345 *Spartan dogs and Cretan quiver:* The Libyan ('African') herdsman carries equipment hard to come by at his latitude, but the mention of Sparta (via the Spartan city Amyclae) and Crete connects this alien figure with the tenacity of those Greek provinces.

349 *Lake Maeotis:* We move now to northern climes, near the Black Sea.

372 *nor by spooking with strands of red feathers:* A rope or cord strung with brightly coloured feathers was stretched across openings at the edge of the wood, to startle game back into the forest and direct the course of their flight.

380 *sour service-berries:* Not being grapes, these produce 'pretend' wine at best.

392 *charmed Luna:* Pan attracted the moon by disguising himself within the dazzling fleece of a ram.

401 *press:* To make cheese. Morning milk is made into cheese at night. Evening milk is taken to market in the morning, or salted for preservation.

405 *Spartan pups and fierce Molossians:* These two breeds of dog make famously good watchdogs.

408 *banditos:* Virgil uses the term *Hiberos* disparagingly, with the suggestion that Spaniards are bandits.

425 *that dire serpent in Calabrian dells:* The amphibious *chersydrus*, which feeds mainly on fish and frogs, can grow to over three feet long and can be found in water even miles out to sea.

463 *swills milk curdled with horse blood:* Virgil's implication is that the practices of these northern tribes show the safety of opening a vein. Virgil uses less familiar names for the peoples in question: *Bisaltae* for a Macedonian tribe, *Geloni* for Scythians, and *Getae* for a Thracian band living on the western shore of the Black Sea.

482 *Nor was the way to death unvarying:* That is, the plague carries symptoms of thirst and fever as well as watery bloat.

526 *no Massic indulgence:* The bullock succumbs despite his adherence to the georgic principles of pure and honourable labour, and his abstinence from luxuriance. See note on 2.143.

531–2 *cattle rounded up / from the back-country:* Because the domestic herds were ravaged by plague.

533 *oxen wild, outsized:* In contrast to the carefully bred and tended white oxen normally used for the sacrificial rites associated with Juno's feast days, these beasts are too big for the chariot.

552 *Plague and Fear:* Harrowing figures from the Underworld, their personified names literally translated from the Latin.

BOOK FOUR

Virgil's final book covers beekeeping, and retells the story of Orpheus and Eurydice.

1 *honey from the sky:* Honey was thought to fall from heaven as dew.

15 *Procne:* The swallow. See glossary note on Procne.

21 *new kings:* Virgil assumes that the hive's queen is male.

35 *narrow entrances:* To keep out extremes of weather as well as intruders.

47 *yew:* Poisonous. See note on 2.257.

48 *the redding crab:* Its odour was considered fatal to bees by Pliny the Elder in his *Naturalis Historia (Natural History)* 11.62.

64 *Mother Cybele's cymbals:* Though Virgil doesn't mention this *Mater* by name, her identity is apparent in the cymbals, which were involved in the worship of the goddess.

111 *Priapus of the Hellespont:* Like scarecrows, phallic wooden figures of the fertility god were placed in gardens. Priapus, who was originally worshipped in Lampsacus, near the Hellespont, was often depicted holding a sickle.

112 *pines:* Bees use pine-gum as propolis to build hives.

119 *Paestum:* The rose gardens of Paestum, in Lucania, were famous, though perhaps not the site of such wondrous – and probably fictitious – double-bloomings.

125 *Tarentum:* Virgil calls it *Oebaliae . . . arcis*, the 'Oebalian citadel'. Oebalus was a king of Sparta, and Tarentum was founded by Spartans.

127 *Corycian:* Corycus is a city in Cilicia, but Virgil may also intend a reference to the Corycian cave on the Muses' Mount Parnassus, shelter of the giant Typhoeus.

144–6 *mature the elms . . . shade for carouses:* The old man is nursing trees to an advanced stage of growth before transplanting them.

149–52 *what nature . . . a Dictaean cave:* Divining that one of his children would depose him, Saturn devoured them as they were born. Jupiter, however, was concealed by his mother in a cave on Mount Dicte in Crete. The Curetes drowned out his infant cries by clashing their shields, preventing Saturn from discovering him. The bees, which Virgil suggests were attracted by the sound, came to the cave and nurtured him with honey, for which service Jupiter endowed them with the social properties described here.

177 *Athenian bees:* Virgil uses the term *Cecropias . . . apes* or 'Cecropian bees'. The reference is to Cecrops, an early Athenian king.

198 *they indulge not in lovemaking:* Virgil's description of bee reproduction – that females accomplish it all by themselves – may not be a biologically sound theory, but it does provide an industrious contrast with the herds of Book Three, which needed to be forcibly restrained from sex in order to perform their duties.

202 *tiny citizens:* Virgil uses the term *Quirites,* which refers specifi-
cally to citizens of Rome, to complete his anthropomorphic vision
of the hive as an industrious society.

230 *spritz and freshen your mouth:* That is, to improve your breath.
Bees, the poem has already suggested, are sensitive to smell (see
4.48–49).

231–8 *Their rage . . . wintry waves:* The order of these lines varies in
different manuscripts. In some versions, the sentence that begins
'Their rage surpasses measure' *follows* the sentence that begins
'Twice men gather the lavish yield.' However, line 230 describes
techniques for moderating the bees' rage, which leads naturally
into a consideration of that rage. Moreover, line 239 continues
with tasks associated with a harsh winter, a logical progression
from the winter (second) harvest of honey discussed here in lines
237–238.

235 *Pleiad Taygete:* The Pleiades star-cluster rises in mid-June and
sets in early November – around the same time that Pisces, and
rainy weather, appear.

246 *the spider spited by Minerva:* Arachne beat Minerva in a weaving
contest, for which the goddess changed her into a spider.

269 *Psithian vine:* The geographic provenance of this wine-grape is
not known.

270 *Athenian thyme:* Grown on Mount Hymettus. Virgil's Latin
references Cecrops, an early Athenian king.

271 *amellus:* This flower is etymologically appropriate to the bees,
since it evokes the Greek μέλιττα, which denotes both bee and
honey, as does the River Mella (line 278).

283 *the Arcadian master:* Aristaeus, son of Apollo and the nymph
Cyrene, although his name doesn't appear in the text until 4.317.
(See note on 1.14.)

284–5 *the spoiled blood from slain bullocks / has often engendered
bees:* This (purely fantastical) technique of spontaneous genera-
tion is called *bugonia.*

287 *Pellaean Canopus:* Alexander's general Ptolemy, who came from
Macedonian Pella, became ruler of Egypt.

290 *quivered Persia's territory:* Virgil refers to eastern cultures gener-
ally, and probably has the famed Parthian bowmen in mind (see
4.314, and 3.31 and note).

291 *swart Indians:* Virgil may be thinking of either Ethiopia or India
as the source of the Nile.

336–45 *Drymo and Xantho . . . Clymene:* Virgil's catalogue of nymphs is in part drawn from Greek and Roman sources, and in part invented from suggestive Greek words.

338 This translation omits a spurious line that appears here in some manuscripts, listing four additional nymphs: *Nesaee Spioque Thaliaque Cymodoceque*. This line is suspiciously like a similar list in the *Iliad*, 18.39–40, and may have been imported from that source.

340 *suffered her first birth-pangs:* Virgil's Latin uses the name of the childbirth goddess Lucina to indicate the birth-pains.

345–6 *the frustrate vigilance / of Vulcan:* Vulcan caught his wife Venus in bed with Mars.

371 *Eridanus, both horns on his bullish front gilt:* River-gods were often represented as horned bulls, due to the bellowing sound of a rushing river. The other rivers mentioned by Virgil provide geographical reach to the catalogue, as if Aristaeus has a divinely far-reaching prospect.

379 *Panchaian flame:* Arabian incense.

387 *Neptune's Carpathian depths:* That is, in the waters surrounding the island Carpathos, near Crete.

454–6 *Heartbroken Orpheus stirs up / these punishments against you (did not Fate intervene) – / far less than your deserving! – :* Proteus' sense of outrage seems to derive from his sense that, though Eurydice's death was technically accidental, Aristaeus' unbridled lust – a force which has ravaged animal populations in Book Three – is its root cause.

467 *Taenarus:* On the southern tip of the Peloponnesus, thought to be the site of a portal to the Underworld.

481–2 *Death's inmost / Tartarus:* Virgil personifies Death in the Latin *Leti*, and gives it dominion over the darkest part of the Underworld.

502 *ferryman of Orcus:* Charon, the boatman, who ferries souls of the dead across to the gates of Tartarus.

505 *Hades:* Virgil does not use this Greek name for the Underworld, but rather calls it *Manes*, a general term for the lower world. Orpheus' sobs must persuade the Underworld particularly as expressed in its primary deity, Pluto (Greek Hades).

520 *Thracian dames:* Virgil refers to the Cicones, inhabitants of southern Thrace.

524 *river of his father's realm:* Virgil calls it *Oeagrius Hebrus*, referring to Orpheus' father Oeagrus, a king of Thrace.

560–61 *while Caesar the Great thundered in war / beside the deep*

Euphrates: Octavian waged war with the Parthians in Asia Minor, and with other eastern peoples, after the Battle of Actium in 31 BC.

562 *pursued his course to heaven:* Continuing the activity described at 1.23–42.

563 *Parthenope:* Naples, to which Virgil fled to escape the strife of civil wars. Virgil studied Epicureanism in Naples, and was given a house there by Maecenas. The *Georgics* was composed in Naples.

565 *shepherd songs:* The *Eclogues.* Line 566 echoes almost exactly the first line of Eclogue 1, in which the shepherd Tityrus recounts to Meliboeus (who has not been so fortunate) how he has regained his confiscated lands.

Glossary

Abydos: A town on the eastern side of the Hellespont, famed for its oysters.

Acerrae: A town in Campania, apparently deserted.

Achelous: A river in central Greece, thought to be the world's oldest river.

Acheron: In the Underworld, the river of woe, piloted by the boatman Charon.

Achilles: Greek hero who was instrumental in the overthrow of Troy, and the central warrior-figure of the *Iliad*.

Acte: An old name for Attica, the region where Athens lies.

Adriatic Sea: Separates Italy (on the west) from the Balkan Peninsula (on the east).

Aegean Sea: Borders Greece on the east.

Aetna: An active volcano on the eastern coast of Sicily.

Alburnus: A mountain in southern Italy, near the valley of the River Tanager.

Alcinous: King of the Phaeacians, famed for his gardens.

Alexander the Great: King of Macedon who lived from 356 to 323 BC and, leading the Greek army, conquered most of the world known at that time, eastward well into India.

Alpheus: A Peloponnesian river, near Olympia.

Alps: A mountain range along the northern border of Italy, stretching from the Mediterranean Sea to the Danube.

Ameria: A region in central Italy, evidently known for its willows.

Aminnean: Grapevine variety grown in Campania.

Amphrysus: A river in Thessaly, in north-eastern Greece, dear to Apollo.

Amyclae: A city under Spartan control.

Amythaon: Father of the Seer Melampus.

Anguis: 'The Snake', also called Draco, constellation half-circling the North Star.

Anio: A river in central Italy, tributary of the Tiber.

Aonian Mountain: See **Helicon**.

Apollo: Son of Jupiter and Leto (Latin *Latona*), born with his twin sister Diana on the island of Delos, Apollo is the far-shooting archer-god, the god of light often associated with the sun, and master of poetry and music, playing a golden lyre. His shrine at Delphi housed Greece's most revered oracle.

Aquarius: The water-bearer, a constellation that sets in February.

Aquilo: See **Boreas**.

Arabia: Then as now, the vast desert peninsula bordered on the west by the Red Sea, on the south-east by the Arabian Sea, and on the north-east by the Persian Gulf.

Arachne: A mortal girl who enraged the goddess Minerva by besting her in a weaving contest. Quailing before Minerva's fury, Arachne hanged herself, and Minerva, repentant, changed her into a spider.

Arcadia: A region in southern Greece, in the Peloponnese, associated with pastures and pastoral song.

Arctos: The constellation Ursa Major, the 'Great Bear'. After Callisto, the daughter of the Arcadian king Lycaon, was impregnated by Jupiter she was turned into a bear by jealous Juno, then killed by a hunting party. Jupiter placed her among the stars.

Arcturus: The brightest star in the constellation Boötes and the third brightest star in the night sky. It rises in springtime.

Arethusa: Once a huntress and follower of Diana, Arethusa was pursued by the river-god Alpheus, who loved her. She ran, but the god had more endurance. Weary, she cried to Diana, who changed her into a spring of water and channelled her from Greece to Sicily, where the spring Arethusa lies in Ortygia. In the *Georgics*, she is a water nymph and companion to Cyrene.

Argitis: A variety of white wine.

Ariadne: Daughter of Minos, of Crete, whose crown was placed in the sky by Bacchus, who loved her.

Aristaeus: Son of Apollo and the nymph Cyrene, beekeeper and master herdsman of Arcadia.

Ascanius: A river in Bithynia, in what is now Turkey.

Ascra: A town in northern Greece and home to Hesiod, the author of *Works and Days*, whose influence is felt throughout the *Georgics*.

Assaracus: Grandfather of Anchises, who fathered Aeneas with Venus.

Assyria: Once an empire that dominated northern Mesopotamia.

Astraea: Daughter of Jupiter, whose name means Justice. During the Saturnian Golden Age she dwelt on earth, but at its end she was the last divine being to tread upon the earth, before being transformed into the constellation Virgo.

Athens: In ancient Greece, a powerful city-state and centre of arts and philosophy.

Athos: Mountain on the Athos Peninsula, in north-eastern Greece.

Atlas: One of the Titans; after their defeat by Zeus, Atlas was ordered to stand at the edge of the earth and uphold the sky on his shoulders. He was also the father of the Pleiades and Hyades.

Attica: A region of Greece which includes Athens.

Aurora: Goddess of the sunrise. She asked Jupiter to make her beloved Tithonus immortal, but forgot to ask that he be eternally young.

Ausonians: Primitive Italians, hailing from Campania.

Auster: The southwind.

Avernus: A crater lake in Campania, Italy, north of Naples, where an entrance into the Underworld was rumoured to lie.

Bacchus: God of wine and the vine, and of fertility. In the *Georgics* he is also called **Lyaeus, Liber, Lenaios** and **Iacchus.**

Bactria: A region in western Asia, north of modern Iran.

Balearic Islands: Located in the western Mediterranean Sea, near modern Spain.

Bear, The: See **Arctos.**

Benacus: The modern Lake Garda, in northern Italy.

Beroe: A nymph, companion to Cyrene.

Bisaltae: A Macedonian tribe on the Strymon river, in Thrace.

Boötes: 'The Herdsman', a northern constellation containing the star Arcturus.

Boreas: The northwind.

Britons: Inhabitants of the modern British Isles, then a Roman colony called Britannia.

Bumast: Grapevine variety known for its burgeoning fruit.

Busiris: Egyptian king whose practice was to sacrifice strangers, for which Hercules slew him.

Caesar: Virgil speaks of two different Caesars in the *Georgics*. At 1.466 he refers to the death of Julius Caesar (100–44 BC), who led the nascent Roman Empire until his assassination by senators hoping to restore republican government. Otherwise, Virgil means Octavian, later Caesar Augustus (63 BC–AD 14), Julius Caesar's adopted son and heir, the first declared emperor of the Roman Empire and advisee of Virgil's patron, Maecenas.

Caicus: A river now called the Bakir, in Mysia (now north-western Turkey).

Calabria: In ancient times the south-easternmost part of Italy, the 'heel'.

Callisto: Daughter of the Arcadian king Lycaon; when Jupiter pursued her, she was turned into a bear by jealous Juno. See **Arctos**.

Camillus: Marcus Furius Camillus (446–365 BC) was a Roman soldier and statesman.

Campania: A region of south-western Italy encompassing Naples, bordered on the west by the Tyrrhenian Sea.

Canis: See **Dog Star**.

Canopus: A city on the western edge of the Nile Delta, in Egypt.

Capitoline Hill: The highest of Rome's seven hills, and storage place for public records.

Capua: An ancient city in Campania, east of Rome and north of Naples.

Carpathos: An island in the Aegean Sea, between Rhodes and Crete.

Castalia: The inspirational spring on the Muses' Mount Parnassus.

Castor: See **Pollux**.

Caucasus: A mountain range that divides Asia and Europe.

Caurus: The north-westwind.

Cayster: A river in Ephesus, in Asia Minor (modern Turkey), which flows into the Aegean Sea.

Cea: An island in the Aegean Sea, also called Ceos, where Aristaeus kept his flocks and bees.

Cecrops: Legendary first king of Athens, who in some myths is imagined as half-man, half-serpent.

Celeus: King of Eleusis, the centre of a vast agricultural religion, and father of Triptolemus.

Centaurs: Half-man, half-horse; largely represented as savage creatures, except Chiron, who was famed for his wisdom.

Ceraunia: A region to the north and west of Greece, now Acroceraunia, Albania.

Cerberus: A giant three-headed dog with the tail of a snake, which guarded the gates of Hades to keep the dead inside, and the living out.

Ceres: Roman goddess of grain crops and agriculture. Often depicted holding sheaves of wheat and poppies.

Chalybes: Inhabitants of the iron-producing region of Chalybia, on the southern shore of the Black Sea in modern Turkey.

Chaonia: A region of north-western Greece, in whose oak-groves stood the ancient oracle of Jupiter (Zeus) at Dodona.

Chaos: A formless confusion preceding the birth of Earth and Heaven.

Charon: The boatman who ferries souls into the Underworld.

Chelae: 'The Claws', the ancient Greek name for the constellation Scorpio.

Chios: An island in the Aegean Sea.

Chiron: A Centaur, the son of the nymph Phillyra and Saturn, who was disguised as a horse during his conception. Renowned for his wisdom and facility with healing arts.

Cicones: A tribe of southern Thrace.

Cilicia: Southern coastal region of Asia Minor.

Cinyps: A river flowing through Libya into the Mediterranean.

Clanius: A river in Campania, given to seasonal flooding.

Clio: A nymph, companion to Cyrene.

Clitumnus: A river in Umbria.

Clymene: A nymph borrowed from Homer, companion to Cyrene.

Cnossus: An ancient city on Crete, the centre of the empire of Minos.

Cocytus: In the Underworld, the river of lamentation.

Coeus: One of the Titans, a son of Ouranos and Gaia, the Sky and the Earth.

Colchis: An ancient kingdom in the Caucasus, where Jason (with the Argonauts, his companions on their ship, the *Argos*) ended his journey and seized the dragon-guarded Golden Fleece, to recover the usurped throne of Thessaly.

Como: A lake in the north of Italy, called the Larius in Virgil's time.

Corinth: A city-state on the Isthmus of Corinth, the stretch of land that joins the Peloponnese to mainland Greece. Corinth oversaw the manufacture of a highly refined bronze.

Corona: 'The Crown' of Ariadne, a northern constellation.

Corycus: A city in Cilicia, in what is now Turkey.

Crassus: Marcus Licinius Crassus (*c.* 115–53 BC), wealthy Roman general and eventual governor of Syria; his troops were defeated in 53 BC by the Parthians, who killed him when he came to their camp to parley.

Crustumerium: An ancient city in the west of Italy, praised for its varieties of pear.

Curetes: Priests of Cybele, also called Corybantes, who lived in Crete.

Cybele: A goddess of Asia Minor who, because of her connection with the earth and fertility, was often associated with Ceres or Rhea, Ceres' mother. Her devotees, the Corybantes, celebrated her in loud ceremonies with drums and cymbals.

Cyclopes: One-eyed giants who lived in a cave in Mount Aetna, in Sicily. Master ironsmiths, they forged Jupiter's lightning bolts.

Cydippe: A nymph, companion to Cyrene.

Cyllarus: A horse given to the brothers Castor and Pollux, both sons of Leda, by their stepmother Juno.

Cyllenius: The planet Mercury, so called because Mercury was born on Mount Cyllene in Arcadia.

Cynthia: A mountain in Delos, birthplace of Apollo.

Cyprus: A Mediterranean island, the birthplace of Venus.

Cyrene: A nymph who lived in the River Peneus, mother to Aristaeus.

Cythaeron: A Theban mountain famous for hunting and for bacchic revels.

Cytorus: A city and mountain in Paphlagonia, in northern Asia Minor.

Dacia: A large region north of the Danube, taking in modern Romania and beyond.

Danube: A river extending from Germany to the Black Sea.

Dawn: See **Aurora**.

Decius: The Decius family distinguished themselves in Roman military and political affairs during the fourth and third centuries BC. Publius Decius Mus (*d.* 340 BC?) led the Roman army during the First Samnite War (343–341 BC), and was famed for his wiles and heroism. He later became a Roman consul (or magistrate). His son was Publius Decius Mus (*d.* 295 BC) who, like his father, served many terms as consul and died in battle. A third-generation Publius Decius Mus (*d.* 279 BC?), grandson and son (respectively) of these renowned Decii, served as consul and led troops in the Battle of Asculum (279 BC) against Pyrrhus of Epirus.

Deiopea: A nymph, companion to Cyrene.

Delos: An Aegean island where Latona gave birth to Apollo and Diana.

Delphi: A shrine on the foothills of Mount Parnassus, which housed Apollo's oracle.

Demeter: Greek equivalent of Ceres.

Deucalion: Son of Prometheus, he and his wife Pyrrha were the only survivors of the Deluge, or Great Flood, and repopulated the earth by sowing stones into the earth.

Diana: Virginal goddess of the hunt and of the Moon, twin sister of Apollo; also called Artemis.

Dicte: A mountain in Crete where Jupiter's mother hid him, so that he wouldn't be eaten by his father Saturn.

Dionysus: See **Bacchus**.

Dis: Another name for **Pluto**.

Dodona: The site of Zeus' ancient oracle in Epirus, in north-western Greece, in a grove of oak trees.

Dog Star: Sirius, the brightest star in the night sky, in the constellation Canis Major, the Great Dog. Its rising in mid-July marked the 'Dog Days' of summer for the Ancient Greeks.

Dryads: Tree nymphs.

Drymo: 'Oak' in Greek; a nymph, companion to Cyrene.

Earth: See **Gaia**.

Eleusis: A Greek city near Athens. The cult of Demeter and Persephone, which was based in Eleusis, celebrated the goddesses in a series of mysteries and cultic rites each year.

Elis: Peloponnesian region that housed Olympia, and thus hosted the Olympic Games.

Elysian Fields: The blessed region of the Underworld, final resting place of virtuous and heroic souls.

Emathia: A region that includes the territories of Thessaly and Macedonia.

Enipeus: A tributary of the Peneus, in Thessaly.

Eoae Atlantides: Literally, 'Daughters of Atlantis', a name for the Pleiades.

Eous: The morning star – that is, the planet Venus; also used by Virgil to designate the East generally.

Ephialtes: Giant son of Neptune, who, with his brother Otus, tore up mountains, and piled them high, and climbed up in an attempt to storm Mount Olympus.

Ephyre: A nymph, companion to Cyrene.

Ephyreia: An ancient name for Corinth.

Epirus: A region that stretched across portions of north-western Greece and modern Albania, to the Ionian Sea, famous for the breeding of good horses.

Erebus: The Underworld.

Erichthonius: King of Athens, credited with inventing the chariot.

Eridanus: The River Po, in northern Italy.

Erigone: The constellation Virgo.

Etruria: A region in west-central Italy, which included modern Tuscany.

Eumenides: See **Furies**.

Euphrates: A great river of Mesopotamia, running from modern Turkey to the Persian Gulf.

Eurus: The eastwind.

Eurydice: Wife of Orpheus.

Eurystheus: King of Mycenae, who imposed on Hercules his Twelve Labours.

Falernia: A region in Campania, south of Rome, that produced strong, expensive and highly regarded wines.

Fauns: Goat-legged men, like Pan, associated with the care of herds.

Forum: The business and legal centre of Rome.

Furies: Three goddesses, inhabitants of the Underworld, who punished transgressors: Alecto ('ceaseless'), Megaera ('grudging') and Tisiphone ('avenging murder').

Gaia: Primordial Greek goddess, the great earth mother, who gave birth to Ouranos, the sky, and then partnered with him to produce the Ocean, the Titans and Kronos (Roman Saturn).

Galaesus: A river in southern Italy.

Ganges: A river in the north of India.

Gargara: A city in the legendarily fertile, mountainous region of the Troad or Biga Peninsula in the north-west of modern Turkey.

Geloni: A Scythian tribe in what is now southern Russia.

Germany: In Virgil's time, Germany's territory extended north of the Danube and east of the Rhine.

Getae: A Thracian tribe, living near the Danube.

Glaucus: Two figures by this name are mentioned in the *Georgics*. The first, at 1.437, is a sea-deity, loved of fishermen. At 3.267 Virgil refers to the Corinthian king who was killed by his horses.

Haedi: Latin name for the constellation the Kids (envisioned as three goats), which rises in the spring and sets in September.

Haemus: A mountain in Thrace, north of Greece on the Balkan Peninsula.

Hebrus: A river in Thrace, north of Greece.

Helicon: A mountain in Greece, just inland from the Gulf of Corinth, sacred to the Muses, whose temple stood on the mountain.

Helios: Sun god.

Hellespont: Modern Dardanelles, the channel connecting the Black Sea to the Mediterranean Sea.

Hercules: Heroic son of Jupiter, renowned for great strength, who had to perform twelve impossible labours as penance for an act of violence.

Hermus: A river flowing through Lydia, in what is now western Turkey.

Hero: A maiden, perhaps a priestess of Aphrodite, beloved of Leander. When he drowned while swimming across the Hellespont to be with her, she threw herself from a tower in despair.

Hippodamia: Wife of Pelops, after she helped him win a chariot race against her father's immortal horses, gifts from Mars.

Hister: The lower Danube.

Hyades: A star cluster in the constellation of Taurus. Five daughters of Atlas and half-sisters of the Pleiades, they wept over the death of their brother Hylas so profusely that they were transformed into stars, which, setting in May and rising in November, were associated with rain.

Hydaspes: A river that flows into the Indus, in India.

Hylaeus: One of the Centaurs who got drunk at the wedding feast of Pirithous and tried to carry off the women.

Hylas: A youth taken by Hercules on the *Argo* to be his armour-bearer, who was carried off by nymphs while drawing water. Hercules, in grief, abandoned his comrades in the quest for the Golden Fleece.

Hymen: God of marriage.

Hymettus: A mountain near Athens, particularly renowned for its thyme, and for its bees and honey.

Hypanis: A river in Scythia, which divides Europe and Asia and flows into the Black Sea.

Hyperborean: Of the far north.

Iacchus: See **Bacchus**.

Iapetus: One of the Titans, a son of Ouranos and Gaia, the Sky and the Earth.

Iapydes: People inhabiting a coastal region of the north-eastern Adriatic Sea, in what was part of the Roman province of Illyria.

Ida: This name is given to two separate mountains. One is the mountain in Crete where Jupiter was raised; the other is in Phrygia, Turkey, and is sacred to Cybele.

Idumaea: Greek form of Edom, a region near the Dead Sea.

Illyria: A region in the west of the Balkan Peninsula.

Inachus: A river-god and father of Io.

India: For Virgil this term seems to indicate the vast reaches to the east of the Roman Empire, including perhaps China and Arabia, as well as India proper.

Indigetes: Roman gods, deified national heroes.

Ino: Queen of Thebes, mother of Melicertes.

Io: A mortal princess, daughter of Inachus, turned into a white heifer by Jupiter to avoid being caught with her by jealous Juno.

Ionian Sea: Borders Greece on the west.

Iphimedia: Queen of Aloeus, who seduced Poseidon (or Neptune) by wading in the sea, and became pregnant with the giants Otus and Ephialtes.

Ismarus: A mountain near the Aegean coast in Thrace, north of Greece.

Iturians: Possibly, peoples of Parthia, famed for their skill with arrows.

Ixion: A ruthless king of Thessaly. After trying to seduce Juno, he was chained to a wheel endlessly turning in Hades.

Jove: The chief Roman god, who ruled the sky with his powerful thunderbolt. Virgil refers to him throughout the *Georgics* as the Father, as Heaven or the sky itself, or more simply as God.

Juno: Daughter of Saturn, wife of Jupiter, patron goddess of marriage and of Rome, where festivals were held at which livestock were slaughtered in her honour.

Jupiter: Another name for Jove.

Justice: See **Astraea**.

Kronos: See **Saturn**.

Lagean: A variety of wine, presumably quick-ripening.

Lampsacus: An ancient Greek city on the eastern side of the Hellespont, and an early centre of Priapus-worship.

Laomedon: King of Troy, father of Priam, and grandfather of Aeneas.

Lapiths: People of Thessaly and (owing to a drunken brawl at Pirithous' wedding feast) enemies of the Centaurs.

Lares: Roman household gods.

Larius: See **Como**.

Latona: Daughter of Titans and the mother of Apollo and Diana. Pregnant and abandoned by Jupiter, she wandered the world seeking shelter and finally gave birth to the twins on the Aegean island of Delos.

Leander: A young man from Abydos, on the eastern side of the Hellespont, who fell in love with Hero, a maiden of Sestos, on the western side of the Hellespont. He drowned while swimming to be with his beloved.

Lenaios: See **Bacchus**.

Lesbos: An island located in the north-eastern Aegean Sea.

Lethe: In the Underworld, the river of forgetfulness, often imagined with poppies and other sleep-inducing plants along its banks.

Letum: Death personified.

Liber: See **Bacchus**.

Libya: A region in northern Africa.

Ligea: 'Clear-voiced' in Greek; a nymph, companion to Cyrene.

Liguria: A coastal region of north-western Italy.

Lucania: An ancient region of southern Italy.

Lucifer: 'The light-bearer'; see **Eous**.

Lucina: Goddess of childbirth.

Lucrine: A lake in Campania, near Naples, connected by a man-made canal to Lake Avernus.

Luna: Goddess of the Moon, also called Phoebe.

Lyaeus: See **Bacchus**.

Lycaeus: A mountain in Arcadia, home to a sanctuary of Pan.

Lycaon: Father of Callisto. See **Arctos**.

Lycorias: A nymph, companion to Cyrene.

Lycus: A river in what is now northern Turkey, flowing into the Black Sea.

Lydia: An ancient kingdom in what is now western Turkey.

Macedonia: A region north of Greece on the Balkan Peninsula.

Maecenas: Gaius Clinius Maecenas (70–8 BC), adviser to Octavian (who would become the first Emperor of Rome as Caesar Augustus) and patron of Virgil. The *Georgics* is addressed to him.

Maenalus: A mountain in Arcadia, sacred to Pan.

Maeonia: A part of Lydia, in Asia Minor.

Maeotis: Not a lake, in fact, but the small modern Sea of Azov, north of the Black Sea, to which it is linked by a small strait.

Maia: One of the Pleiades, and mother of Mercury.

Manes: Souls of the dead; the term is sometimes extended to the Underworld generally.

Mantua: The town of Virgil's birth, in the north of Italy; much of the region's land was commandeered by Octavian and reassigned to war veterans.

Mareotis: A lake south of Alexandria, in Egypt.

Marius: Gaius Marius, Roman general and statesman (157–86 BC), who reformed the Roman military.

Mars: Roman god of war.

Marsians: Ancient inhabitants of Marsi, in central Italy.

Massicus: A mountain in central Italy, famous for its wine-grapes.

Media: An empire in what is now north-west Iran, home to the Medes.

Megara: A trade port south of Athens, in Greece.

Melampus: A famed soothsayer, with the ability to understand animal speech.

Melicertes: A mortal changed into the god of harbours after being thrown into the sea by his mother Ino, who was trying to save him from his insane father.

Mella: A river north of the Po, into which it flows.

Mercury: Roman messenger god, for whose speed the fast-moving planet was named.

Mesopotamia: An ancient region between the Tigris and Euphrates rivers.

Methymna: A town on the Aegean island of Lesbos.

Milesian wool: A product of Miletus, an ancient city on the west coast of modern Turkey, known for its luxurious cloth.

Mincius: A river flowing out of Lake Benacus, through Virgil's native Mantua, and into the Po.

Minerva: Roman goddess of wisdom (equivalent to Greek Athena), credited with inventing the olive.

Minos: King of Crete and other Aegean islands, loved by Scylla.

Molorchus: A shepherd in whose cottage Hercules rested before killing the Nemean lion. The lion had killed Molorchus' son.

Molossian: Refers to the descendants of Molossus, a people who settled in Epirus after the fall of Troy. Their vicious dogs were prized as watchdogs.

Moon: See **Luna**.

Muses: Nine sisters, daughters of Jupiter, who were thought to live on Mount Parnassus and Mount Helicon. Goddesses of the arts.

Mycenae: Peloponnesian town.

Mysia: A legendarily fertile region in the north-west of ancient Asia Minor, now Turkey.

Napaeae: Nymphs of glens and groves.

Naryx: A region of resettled Greeks in southern Italy.

Nemea: Peloponnesian site where Hercules killed the Nemean lion, one of his Twelve Labours.

Neptune: The god of the seas and brother of Jupiter; credited with creating the horse.

Nereus: A minor sea-god and father of the Nereids (sea nymphs).

Niphates: Part of Armenia's Taurus mountain range.

Nisus: King of Megara, and father of Scylla, who had a lock of purple hair that rendered him invincible.

Noricum: An ancient region in what is now Austria.

Notus: See **Auster**.

Nymphs: Minor goddesses, female spirits associated with particular locations.

Ocean: A Titan, lord of the great river that encircled the earth. Husband of Tethys, with whom he sired all river-nymphs and river-gods.

Octavian: See **Caesar**.

Oeagrus: King of Thrace and father of Orpheus.

Oebalus: King of Sparta.

Olympia: A sanctuary in Elis, in the north-west Peloponnesian peninsula in southern Greece, the site of the Olympic Games.

Olympus: The highest mountain in Greece, considered to be the home of the gods.

Opis: A nymph, companion to Cyrene.

Orcus: Another name for Pluto, god of the Underworld (called Hades by the Greeks).

Oriens: See **Aurora**.

Orithyia: Daughter of Erechtheus, king of Athens. When the north-wind, Boreas, fell in love with her, he gusted upon her and carried her away.

Orpheus: Son of the muse Calliope and Oeagrus, king of Thrace; most skilled of singers. When his wife Eurydice was killed, Orpheus went to the Underworld and persuaded Hades, by the power of his song, to let her return to earth – provided he did not turn around to look at her on the journey back.

Ossa: A mountain in Thessaly, in north-eastern Greece.

Otus: Giant son of Neptune, who, with his brother Ephialtes, tore up mountains, and piled them high, and climbed up in an attempt to storm Mount Olympus.

Ouranos: Greek sky-god, the son and husband of Gaia and, with her, father of the Titans. The youngest Titan, Kronos (Roman Saturn), ambushed, castrated and deposed Ouranos, and ushered in the idyllic Golden Age.

Paestum: A town in southern Italy, famous for its rose gardens.

Palatine: The first-settled of Rome's seven hills, and the residential area for distinguished Romans, including several emperors.

Pales: Goddess of herds and flocks.

Pallas Athena: See **Minerva**.

Pallene: A Thracian headland jutting into the north of the Aegean Sea.

Pan: Arcadian god of flocks and woodlands, the half-goat son of Hermes.

Panchaia: A legendarily fertile oasis or island, perhaps *only* legendary, but associated by some with Arabia.

Pangaea: A mountain in Macedonia, north of Greece.

Panope: One of the Nereids or sea nymphs.

Paphos: A town on the Mediterranean island of Cyprus; mythical birthplace of Venus.

Parnassus: A mountain in central Greece, sacred to Apollo, and home to the Muses.

Paros: An island in the Aegean Sea, famous for its fine white marble, which was used for statuary.

Parthenope: One of the Sirens – sea nymphs with enchanting voices – who was supposed to be buried near Naples; thus, Naples is also referred to by this name.

Parthia: An ancient kingdom covering all of modern Iran, and beyond into much of the Middle East.

Pax: Goddess of peace.

Peace: See **Pax**.

Pelethronium: Perhaps in Thessaly, believed to be the habitat of the Centaurs.

Pelion: A mountain in Thessaly.

Pella: A town in Macedonia, north of Greece. Home territory of Ptolemy, ruler of Egypt under Alexander the Great.

Pelops: Husband of Hippodamia, whose hand he won in a chariot race against her father. His father Tantalus killed Pelops and served him cooked to the gods, but Jupiter reconstructed him, without his shoulder, which had been eaten by Ceres.

Penates: Roman household gods.

Peneus: A river that flows through the gorgeous vale of Tempe, in Thessaly; home to the nymph Cyrene. Also, that river's god.

Persephone: See **Proserpina**.

Persia: An ancient empire in western Asia, which saw its vastest reach (roughly from the Black Sea to India) between the fifth and third centuries BC.

Phaeacians: The inhabitants of an island in the Ionian Sea, off the coast of Epirus.

Phasis: A river flowing from the Caucasus Mountains into the Black Sea.

Philippi: A Macedonian town where Octavian (later Caesar Augustus) and Antony achieved victory over the forces aligned behind Brutus and Cassius, in 42 BC.

Phillyra: Mother of the Centaur Chiron.

Phoebe: See **Luna**.

Pholus: One of the Centaurs who, at the wedding feast of Pirithous, got drunk and tried to carry off the women.

Phrygia: Kingdom in the west of the Anatolian plateau, in what is now western Turkey.

Phyllodoce: 'Leaf-receiver' in Greek; a nymph, companion to Cyrene.

Pirithous: Thessalian king whose wedding became the occasion for a brawl between Centaurs and Lapiths.

Pisa: A city in ancient Etruria (modern Tuscany), in north-western Italy.

Pisces: 'The Fish', a constellation.

Pleiades: A star cluster in the constellation of Taurus, also known as the Seven Sisters, daughters of the Titan Atlas and the nymph Pleione, and half-sisters to the Hyades. The Pleiades were pursued by Orion until Zeus, out of pity, turned them into stars. The cluster rises in mid-June, and sets in early November.

Pluto: God of the Underworld, sometimes called Orcus or Dis or, in Greek, Hades.

Po: A major river flowing through northern Italy into the Adriatic Sea.

Pollux: Son of Zeus (Jupiter) and twin brother of Castor. The brothers were revered for their horsemanship, celebrated especially by the Roman cavalry, as well as by the Spartan military.

Pompey: Gnaeus Pompeius Magnus (106–48 BC, Roman military and political leader who, with Marcus Licinus Crassus and Julius Caesar, ruled Rome as the First Triumvirate. After the death of Crassus, Pompey became Caesar's rival for Roman leadership, until he was defeated by Caesar's forces in civil war.

Pontus: The Black Sea.

Potnia: A site in Greece near Thebes where Glaucus kept his team of racing mares.

Priapus: Fertility god, son of Venus and Bacchus, often depicted in phallic-shaped statuary. A shrine to Priapus stood along the Hellespont.

Procne: To make her husband Tereus suffer for his infidelity, Procne killed their son and served him for dinner. Her sister Philomela helped her. As her husband pursued her in rage, Procne was changed into a swallow; the red colouring on the swallow's breast feathers signals her crime. Philomela was changed into a nightingale.

Proserpina: Daughter of Ceres and goddess of spring. Abducted by Pluto for his bride, she was permitted to return to earth for eight months of the year, during which plant life flourished under the happiness of her mother. During the time Proserpina spent in the Underworld, the land was frozen with Ceres' grief.

Proteus: A minor sea-god, son of Neptune. He had the gift of prophecy and could shift his shape.

Psithian: A variety of wine, of unknown provenance

Ptolemy: A Macedonian general (367–283 BC) under Alexander the

Great (356–323 BC), who became ruler of Egypt and founded the Ptolemaic kingdom.

Quirinus: The name of Romulus after he was deified and adopted as a battle-god for later Romans.
Quirites: Roman citizens.

Remus: Co-founder of Rome, with his twin brother Romulus (both sired by Mars).
Rhaetia: A region in the northern Roman Empire, over the Alps from Italy.
Rhesus: King of Thrace, who fought with the Trojans against Greece.
Rhipaean Mountains: A fabled range in the land to the extreme north, beyond Scythia, thought to be eternally snow-covered and shrouded in darkness.
Rhodes: A large island in the eastern Aegean Sea.
Rhodope: A mountain to the north of Greece, in Thrace.
Rhoetus: One of the Centaurs who, at the wedding feast of Pirithous, got drunk and tried to carry off the women.
Romulus: Co-founder of Rome, with his twin brother Remus (both sired by Mars).

Sabaeans: Inhabitants of Saba, a kingdom of the south-west Arabian Peninsula (in what is now Yemen) famous for its incense.
Sabines: Ancient inhabitants of Italy before the founding of Rome.
Sarrano: An old Latin name for Tyre.
Saturn (Greek **Kronos**): The chief of the Titans, who reigned in the age before the Olympian gods. He ruled during the mythic Golden Age, an age of peace and plenty, until he was overthrown by his own son, Jupiter.
Scipio: A martial family of ancient Rome. Publius Cornelius Scipio Africanus Major (236–183 BC) led the Roman armies as a general, and defeated Hannibal, who attacked from Carthage on elephants. Publius Cornelius Scipio Aemilianus (185–129 BC) was the adopted grandson of the elder Scipio; also a Roman general, he led the siege that destroyed Carthage in 146 BC.
Scylla: Daughter of Nisus, king of Megara. She fell in love with Minos, enemy of Nisus, and for his sake cut off the enchanted purple lock of hair from her father's head, causing his city's overthrow by Minos.
Scythia: A vast region in Eurasia, north and north-east of the Black

Sea. The Scythians or Scyths were a nomadic, horse-riding people revered for their toughness.

Sicyon: A Peloponnesian town.

Sila: A forested mountain in Bruttium, in southern Italy.

Silarus: A river in Campania.

Silvanus: Roman god of fields and woodlands, associated with the cypress tree because of his love for Cyparissus, a youth who was transformed by grief into a cypress after he'd inadvertently killed a favourite stag.

Sisyphus: King of Corinth who revealed that Jupiter had carried off a river-nymph and was punished in the Underworld by having to try forever to roll a giant rock uphill, which kept rolling down upon him again.

Sparta: A great warrior city, located in the Peloponnese in southern Greece. It lies to the east of Mount Taygetus.

Spercheus: A river in Thessaly, in north-east Greece.

Strymon: A river in Thrace, north of Greece.

Styx: The boundary-river of the Underworld.

Taburnus: A mountain in the Apennine range, in central Italy.

Taenarus: A site at the southern tip of Greece where a seaside cave was supposed to be an entrance to the Underworld.

Tanager: A river in southern Italy.

Tanais: A river flowing through modern Russia into the Sea of Azor, which Virgil identifies as Lake Maeotis, north and east of the Black Sea.

Tantalus: Son of Zeus who dismembered and cooked his son Pelops, and served him as a sacrifice to the gods. Though Pelops was revivified by Zeus (albeit with an ivory shoulder), Tantalus' Underworld punishment for his affront was to stand in a pool of water under a fruit tree with low branches. Whenever he reached for it, the fruit evaded his grasp. Whenever he bent down to drink, the water receded beyond his reach.

Tarentum: A region in the south-east of Italy, on the Ionian Sea.

Tartarus: The deepest and grimmest part of the Underworld, the dungeon of Hades, roughly equivalent to Hell.

Taurus: 'The Bull' constellation, visible in the northern hemisphere during winter.

Taygete: One of the Pleiades.

Taygetus: A mountain in the Peloponnese, part of which is in Arcadia; it overlooks Sparta.

Tegea: A settlement in ancient Arcadia, a region with a strong pastoral tradition associated with the god Pan.

Tempe: A scenic valley between Olympus and Ossa in Thessaly, in north-eastern Greece.

Tethys: Wife of Ocean and mother of all the nymphs.

Thasos: An island in the northern Aegean Sea.

Thebes: A Greek city to the north and west of Athens.

Theseus: King of Athens, who conquered Thebes, sailed with Jason on the *Argo*, and defeated the Minotaur.

Thetis: One of the fifty Nereids or daughters of the sea-god Nereus, and mother of Achilles.

Thrace: A region that anciently included north-eastern Greece. Its boundaries extended north to the Danube, south to the Aegean Sea and east to the Black Sea.

Thule: A land beyond Britain, proverbially the landfall farthest north, or at the farthest reaches of the navigable world (perhaps, some speculate, the Orkneys, Iceland or Greenland).

Thymbra: A site in modern Turkey, near Troy, the location of a shrine to Apollo.

Tiber: A river whose course runs long through Italy. Rome was founded on its eastern banks.

Tigris: An eastern boundary-river of ancient Mesopotamia, flowing from the Taurus Mountains in what is now Turkey to the Persian Gulf.

Timavus: A river that runs from the mountains of the north-west Balkans into the Adriatic Sea.

Tisiphone: 'Avenging murder', one of the three Furies.

Titans: Giants who ruled the earth until they were overthrown by Jupiter. Jupiter's father, Saturn, was their leader.

Tithonus: Lover of Aurora, the Dawn, who was granted immortality but not eternal youth. He was the brother of Trojan king Priam.

Tityrus: A shepherd, one of the two participants in Virgil's earlier work, the *Eclogues*.

Tmolus: A mountain in Lydia, or Phrygia (modern Turkey).

Triptolemus: Prince of Eleusis, credited with the invention of agriculture.

Tros: Great-grandson of Zeus in the *Iliad*, who sires Ilus (grandfather of Priam) and Assaracus (grandfather of Anchises); his offspring are the House of Troy.

Troy: A city in Asia Minor. Aeneas, son of the Trojan king Priam, fled Troy after it had been sacked by the Greeks and eventually ended up in Italy, where he founded Rome.

Typhoeus: The last and most terrible offspring of Earth, also called Typhon. He was a giant who, rebelling against the rule of Jupiter, was struck by that god's thunderbolt and buried under Mount Aetna.

Tyre: An ancient Phoenician city on the Mediterranean Sea (in what is now Lebanon), famous for the purple dye it extracted from shellfish.

Tyrrhenian Sea: Borders Italy on the west.

Vesper: The evening star.

Vesta: Virgin goddess of home and hearth, who at times lends her name to the hearth itself.

Vesuvius: A volcano above Naples.

Volscians: Ancient inhabitants of the hill-country in central Italy, hostile to Rome. Caesar Augustus was born in Volscian territory.

Vulcan: The blacksmith god of volcanos, son of Jupiter and Juno, and husband to Venus, who cuckolded him (despite his vigilance) with Mars.

Xantho: 'Blonde' in Greek; a nymph, companion to Cyrene.

Zephyr: The westwind, bringer of warmth.

PENGUIN CLASSICS

METAMORPHOSES
OVID

> 'Her soft white bosom was ringed in a layer of bark,
> her hair was turned into foliage, her arms into branches'

Ovid's sensuous and witty poem brings together a dazzling array of mythological tales, ingeniously linked by the idea of transformation – often as a result of love or lust – where men and women find themselves magically changed into new and sometimes extraordinary beings. Beginning with the creation of the world and ending with the deification of Augustus, Ovid interweaves many of the best-known myths and legends of ancient Greece and Rome, including the stories of Daedalus and Icarus, Pyramus and Thisbe, Pygmalion, Perseus and Andromeda, and the Fall of Troy. Erudite but light-hearted, dramatic and yet playful, the *Metamorphoses* has influenced writers and artists throughout the centuries from Shakespeare and Titian to Picasso and Ted Hughes.

This lively, accessible new translation by David Raeburn is in hexameter verse form, which brilliantly captures the energy and spontaneity of the original. The edition contains an introduction discussing the life and work of Ovid as well as a preface to each book, explanatory notes and an index of people, gods and places.

A new verse translation by David Raeburn with an introduction by Denis Feeney

PENGUIN CLASSICS

THE AGRICOLA *AND* THE GERMANIA
TACITUS

> 'Happy indeed were you, Agricola,
> not only in your glorious life but in your timely death'

The Agricola is both a portrait of Julius Agricola – the most famous governor of Roman Britain and Tacitus' well-loved and respected father-in-law – and the first detailed account of Britain that has come down to us. It offers fascinating descriptions of the geography, climate and peoples of the country, and a succinct account of the early stages of the Roman occupation, nearly fatally undermined by Boudicca's revolt in AD 61 but consolidated by campaigns that took Agricola as far as Anglesey and northern Scotland. The warlike German tribes are the focus of Tacitus' attention in *The Germania*, which, like *The Agricola*, often compares the behaviour of 'barbarian' peoples favourably with the decadence and corruption of Imperial Rome.

Harold Mattingly's translation brings Tacitus' extravagant imagination and incisive wit vividly to life. In his introduction, he examines Tacitus' life and literary career, the governorship of Agricola, and the political background of Rome's rapidly expanding Empire. This edition also includes a select bibliography, and maps of Roman Britain and Germany.

Translated with an introduction by H. Mattingly

Translation revised by S. A. Handford

THE STORY OF PENGUIN CLASSICS

Before 1946 ... 'Classics' are mainly the domain of academics and students; readable editions for everyone else are almost unheard of. This all changes when a little-known classicist, E. V. Rieu, presents Penguin founder Allen Lane with the translation of Homer's *Odyssey* that he has been working on in his spare time.

1946 Penguin Classics debuts with *The Odyssey*, which promptly sells three million copies. Suddenly, classics are no longer for the privileged few.

1950s Rieu, now series editor, turns to professional writers for the best modern, readable translations, including Dorothy L. Sayers's *Inferno* and Robert Graves's unexpurgated *Twelve Caesars*.

1960s The Classics are given the distinctive black covers that have remained a constant throughout the life of the series. Rieu retires in 1964, hailing the Penguin Classics list as 'the greatest educative force of the twentieth century.'

1970s A new generation of translators swells the Penguin Classics ranks, introducing readers of English to classics of world literature from more than twenty languages. The list grows to encompass more history, philosophy, science, religion and politics.

1980s The Penguin American Library launches with titles such as *Uncle Tom's Cabin*, and joins forces with Penguin Classics to provide the most comprehensive library of world literature available from any paperback publisher.

1990s The launch of Penguin Audiobooks brings the classics to a listening audience for the first time, and in 1999 the worldwide launch of the Penguin Classics website extends their reach to the global online community.

The 21st Century Penguin Classics are completely redesigned for the first time in nearly twenty years. This world-famous series now consists of more than 1300 titles, making the widest range of the best books ever written available to millions – and constantly redefining what makes a 'classic'.

The Odyssey continues ...

The best books ever written

PENGUIN (🐧) CLASSICS

SINCE 1946

Find out more at www.penguinclassics.com